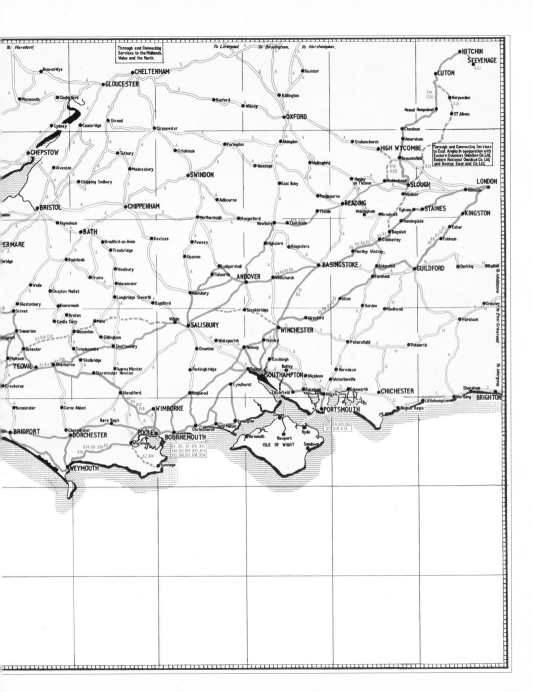

ROYAL BLUE DAYS

COLIN MORRIS

Ian Allan
PUBLISHING

Front cover: Western National No 2244 (623 DDV), a Bristol MW6G/ECW 39-seater of 1960, heads west through Dorchester in July 1971 on a variant of route X10 from Bournemouth to Salcombe, Devon, via Bridport and the Dorset coast — a particularly spectacular journey. A glimpse of a fawn-and-red coach of Bere Regis & District Motor Services — then operating more than 80 vehicles — serves as a reminder of the contribution made by R. W. Toop's firm to weekend express-relief work during this period. *C. L. Caddy*

Back cover: A fully loaded 45-seat Royal Blue RELH6G/ECW coach of 1964, Southern National No 2363 (ATA 105B), makes a brief stop in Farnham, Surrey, on a journey from Bournemouth to London Victoria via Southampton, Winchester and Guildford. The bus stop at which it has come to rest was periodically claimed also by a Southdown express coach coming 'up to town' from Portsmouth. *Mike Stephens*

Title page: Awaiting its driver beside the rustic Royal Blue office at what used to be Southern National's Bridport depot is No 2387 (RDV 413H), bound for Bournemouth on 26 November 1972. A Bristol RELH6G/ECW 45-seat coach, it had been new in 1970, in which year all vehicles delivered were, for the first time, allocated solely to the Western National Omnibus Co Ltd — a situation that would obtain each year thereafter until WNOC's division into smaller units in 1983. *C. L. Caddy*

CONTENTS

First published 2008

ISBN 978 0 7110 3234 7

Published by Ian Allan Publishing

an imprint of Ian Allan Publishing Ltd, Hersham, Surrey, KT12 4RG

Printed in England by Ian Allan Printing Ltd, Hersham, Surrey, KT12 4RG

Code: 0808/B1

Visit the Ian Allan Publishing website at www.ianallanpublishing.com

For
MIKE STEPHENS
in acknowledgement of his amazing generosity and patience

Left: Crewmen in summer uniform swap stories before a row of Bristol LS and MW coaches at Paris Street coach station, Exeter, in the summer of 1968. These are Cornwall-based feeder-service vehicles awaiting the 'big boy' REs from London, Bristol, Bournemouth and elsewhere. From left to right (and, coincidentally, in order of distance to be travelled) they are bound for Looe, Pentreath, Mevagissey and Helston — all destinations off the beaten track. *Mike Stephens*

INTRODUCTION AND ACKNOWLEDGEMENTS

How important is 'myth' — a widely held but false notion? Very, apparently — particularly when historians fail to do their research diligently and reviewers perpetuate the falsity. Thus: 'Mr Elliott at the age of 22 started a horse-drawn coach service to link Bournemouth with the Southampton & Dorchester Railway' — No, he did not! I corrected this notion in *Glory Days: Royal Blue* in 2000 and explained why. If necessary I shall continue to do so until I turn (royal) blue in the face: the link between Holmsley station ('Christchurch Road' in those days) and the Bath Hotel in Bournemouth was started by William Humby, of the King's Arms Hotel, Christchurch, in 1851. (See picture on page 5 of *Glory Days: Bournemouth Transport*.) Thomas Elliott got his first licence (No 217) to drive his uncle's cabs in 1880 and did not possess a vehicle of his own (a four-seat Landau) until October 1885. His first four-in-hand vehicle was licensed in 1888, and the first of his four replica stage coaches he acquired in April 1894 (Licence No 21).

How did this false notion arise? Thomas himself made no such claims — and neither did those who composed his obituary for the local newspapers. When the transport industry locally became motorised at the beginning of the 20th century, however, and competition became fierce, great store was placed by those in trade to be thought the originators of something or other. Whereas nowadays it is rather trendy to be seen as a bright new innovator, in those times 'founded in 1880' (plus a little 'embroidery' to support it) impressed the people who really mattered — the holidaymakers who could be persuaded to join 'your coach' for an excursion, rather than one belonging to one of the numerous competitors also ranged around the stands in The Square, Bournemouth. So, Thomas Elliott's surviving sons, Jack and Harry, decided (unnecessarily, as it turned out) to give their business an added boost by claiming to be 'founded in 1880' (well, that's true, more or less) 'with a coach service linking the Southampton & Dorchester Railway with Bournemouth' (no!), as well as being 'the first in Bournemouth with motor taxicabs' (no!), 'the first with a motor charabanc' (no!) and 'the first with pneumatic tyres on our motor charabancs' (no!). One can understand why the brothers felt it necessary to make these claims at the time, but Jack and Harry Elliott repeated them to anyone who cared to *ask* for the rest of their lives. That's a shame in a way, for, like pedigree race-horses, they'd come through the field and galloped magnificently away and out of sight of their competitors. That was their real achievement! But doubtless the myths will live on.

At the beginning of *Glory Days: Royal Blue* (2000) I gave a short list of *some* operators who from time to time had also used this elegant fleetname. This introduction gives me an opportunity to thank the several readers who wrote to tell me that I 'could have mentioned also …' So, herewith an additional three examples of 'Royal Blues' which again are not the subject of this book — and I emphasise once again that *Royal Blue Days* (2008) is about the Royal Blue started in the late 19th century by Thomas Elliott and whose fleetname was finally dispensed with by Western National Ltd one hundred years later. Principally this volume is about those who organised, drove and travelled in its coaches.

Clement Preece, known in the industry as 'Mr Royal Blue' — he was Traffic Manager (Commercial) of the Southern and Western National companies with special responsibility for Royal Blue — once (1957) wrote that 'When one is asked to produce an article, even on a subject that is fairly familiar, I think it is generally the case that the greatest educative benefit comes not to the reader of the article but to the author.' How true! But I hope you like this book anyway.

There are several people I have to thank for their help and advice in its production, and, inevitably, some of them are the same as those who have kindly contributed toward other volumes I have penned. First, much of the information about the early days of the Elliott brothers' Royal Blue — together with a clutch of sepia photographs — came as a result of an interview in 1957 with Harry Rollings: he had been the general manager of that firm. At about the same time I was able to glean a feminine perspective upon the subject by meeting Mrs J. T. G. Elliott, then living at Lyndhurst. There followed contributions from S. C. Bullock, John Henry, Eric L. Jones, R. Keevil, J. C. Ransom, Douglas Morison and J. T. Wilson.

More recently I have benefited beyond measure through the on-going help received from the researcher who knows more about the history of Royal Blue than anyone else — Peter Delaney, of Wargrave.

I learned much from Colin Billington and from R. J. Crawley of the West Country Historic Omnibus & Transport Trust, whose contributions were of considerable help also. For illustrations I am obliged to Colin Caddy, David Ray and, once again, in particular to Mike Stephens, to whom this book is dedicated.

For their contributions on what I believe to have been the very first 'Royal Blue' coaches I must acknowledge the input of Paul Thomas of Devizes Library, Ben Daubney of Wiltshire & Swindon Archives and, especially, Anne Buchanan of the Local Studies Department in Bath, Somerset. To the names of John Henry and Eric Jones, express drivers of the 'Twenties, it is a pleasure to add those of Royal Blue drivers Jack Eldridge of Wimborne, Doug Fellowes of Poole and David Wride of Bridgwater — and to say a big thankyou to Howard Evans, Philip Emond and Alan Walker, for permitting me to record reminiscences of their earlier careers as express-coach drivers upon Royal Blue, Associated Motorways and National Express routes.

That recording session was organised and hosted at Taunton by Michael Rourke, retired Managing Director of Southern National Ltd, whose important contributions to my last four books have been unwavering.

Finally, my thanks yet again to Andrew Waller and Alan Lambert, whose patience must surely have been stretched to the limit — a sentiment I also extend to the publisher.

Colin Morris
Heswall
April 2008

Note: As fleet lists of Royal Blue motor coaches over the years have been published elsewhere, only those of the relevant horse-drawn vehicles and the early motor taxicabs of Elliott Bros are included in this book. A list of chassis makes and models of vehicles which bore the Royal Blue fleetname is, however, provided, on page 96.

Right: A frosty morning at a military camp 'somewhere on Salisbury Plain' during the first year of World War 2, and soldiers on weekend leave are being picked up by coaches bound for London (Victoria) via Andover and Basingstoke. Supervising this diversion from the usual route is Clem Preece, standing by the door of Beadle-bodied Bristol JJW No 185 (ATT 935) of Southern National. Bringing up the rear are two rebodied ex-Elliott AECs — a Regal and a Reliance. *Colin Morris collection*

1. THE ELLIOTTS' ROYAL BLUE

It is generally accepted that the first regular daily express service operated by road motor vehicles commenced on 11 February 1925. Greyhound Motors Ltd of Bristol provided specially equipped Dennis coaches which ran between that city and London via Bath, Marlborough, Newbury, Reading and Slough along the celebrated 'Great West Road', with time-honoured comfort and refreshment stops along the way. This route was later to be extended to Weston-super-Mare and run jointly from 1928 with Elliott Bros' Royal Blue.

The combination of the names Greyhound and Royal Blue in relation to passenger transport along the Great West Road has a precedent to the above, going back to horse-drawn coaches in the early 19th century — and possibly earlier. For in the late 1820s the Greyhound Hotel, opposite the Guildhall in Market Place, Bath, was the base for a 'Royal Blue' stage-coach service to London — the earliest reference to a passenger-carrying vehicle of that name. Moreover, the eastward journey seems to have been a 'night service', for it departed Bath at 4pm daily (not Sundays) calling *en route*, some 67 miles later, at the Mail Office in Albion Street, Reading, at 1.45 the following morning — a leisurely journey with at least two refreshment stops along the way — one probably at the Pelican (with its 'very large bill') in Newbury. With another 39 miles to reach London it does suggest that at least three vehicles labelled 'Royal Blue' would have been necessary to maintain the routine, together with time set aside to service them.

By 1833, however, 'Royal Blue' had gone from that road, being supplanted by Sarah Ann Mountain & Co's 'The Age' coaches, which departed from The Greyhound at 5pm; maybe they 'performed' (as was said in those days)

somewhat faster. Nevertheless, the fact that there was a 'Royal Blue' coach service running between London and Bath well before the Great Western Railway and the forerunner of the Southern Railway got going is noteworthy, bearing in mind the role which both companies were to play in the provision of Royal Blue express motor coaches more than 100 years later. What is certain, however, is that these Bath-based 'Royal Blues' had no linear connection whatsoever with the replica stage coaches used in Bournemouth from 6 April 1894 by Thomas Elliott , whose choice of 'Royal Blue' as a fleetname was inspired by a horse-bus service he'd seen as a child in his native Stepney. That London fleet had been renamed (from 'Eagle') by John Clark following a gracious personal encounter at Hyde Park Corner with the young Queen Victoria — they had bowed to each other.

The Square, Bournemouth, in 1899, with the Empress Hotel at the bottom of Richmond Hill dominating the backdrop. On the Avenue Road stand an ornate double-chair harnessed to a pony heads two more-conventional examples which are small-horse-drawn. Four landaus are visible: the nearest, hauled by a leggy grey, is about to ascend Commercial Road and two three-horse double-deck buses — one at the entrance to what used to be Sanatorium Road and the other in Gervis Place. There seems to have been no hard-and-fast rule about which way to go around the middle. *Colin Morris collection*

Licensed vehicles operated by George Cutler, of 7 Commercial Road, Bournemouth

Tom Elliott, first licensed to drive PSVs in 1880, would have driven all these vehicles prior to acquiring his own, the first in October 1885. George Cutler died 22 August 1886.

Licence No	Date in	Type	Class	Notes
34	2 November 1878	Double chair	3rd	to Tom Elliott 1887
37	2 November 1878	Bath chair	4th	sold 1892
38	2 November 1878	Bath chair	4th	sold 1892
39	2 November 1878	Bath chair	4th	sold 1892
40	31 August 1880	Double chair	3rd	to W. G. Neville 19 Jan. 1888
70	8 September 1881	Small Brougham	3rd	
103	9 February 1882	Landau	2nd	
174	20 September 1883	Double chair	3rd	to Arthur Neville 19 Jan. 1888
299	18 September 1884	Landau	B	

Licensed vehicles operated by Thomas Elliott, 1885-1910

Licence No	Date in	Type	Class	Notes
380	8 October 1885	Landau	A	
34	April 1887	Double chair	C	ex Cutler
410	30 June 1887	Barouche	A	
28	4 August 1887	?	?	ex Newbery
206	June 1888	Double chair	C	
216	17 June 1888	Landau	A	
213	17 June 1888	Landau	A	
23 (1st use)	17 August 1888	Charabanc	A ‡	19/4
38	18 August 1888	Charabanc	A ‡	
39	18 August 1888	Wagonette	A ‡	
34	4 January 1889	Double chair	C	ex J. Harris
498	29 June 1889	Landau	A	
586	29 June 1889	Landau	A	
3	22 March 1890	Charabanc	A ‡	15/4
54	22 March 1890	Charabanc	A ‡	16/2
85	22 March 1890	Wagonette	A ‡	
129	27 June 1890	Landau	A	
553	27 June 1890	Landau	A	
583	26 September 1890	Brougham	A	
302	19 June 1891	Double chair	C	
305	19 June 1891	Double chair	C	
306	19 June 1891	Landau	A	
509	19 June 1891	Landau	A	
482	19 June 1891	Double chair	C	
97	18 September 1891	Brake	B ‡	12/2
109	25 March 1892	Charabanc	A ‡	
110	25 March 1892	Wagonette	A ‡	
383	April 1892	?	?	ex Frederick Tubbs
679	7 October 1892	Landau	A	
?	24 March 1893	Brake	A ‡	16/2
8	7 July 1893	Landau	A	
11	7 July 1893	Landau	A	
21	7 July 1893	Landau	A	
26	7 July 1893	Landau	A	
36	7 July 1893	Landau	A	
40	7 July 1893	Landau	A	
52	7 July 1893	Landau	A	
356	7 July 1893	Brougham	A	Victoria 1902, landau 1905
188	7 July 1893	Brougham	A	
96	7 July 1893	Barrouche	A	
1	6 April 1894	Brake	A ‡	10/2 October 1908
19	6 April 1894	Charabanc	A ‡	19/4
21	6 April 1894	Coach	A ‡	24/4*
23 (2nd use)	6 April 1894	Charabanc	A ‡	16/2
72	6 April 1894	Brake	A ‡	12/2
73	6 April 1894	Wagonette	A ‡	10/2
17	6 April 1894	Double chair	C	
86 (1st use)	22 March 1895	Wagonette	A ‡	6/1
145	5 July 1895	Landau	A	
357	5 July 1895	Landau	A	
92	20 December 1895	Omnibus	B ‡	5/1
26	25 March 1896	Coach	A ‡	22/4*; ex F. H. Beamish
93	25 March 1896	Omnibus	B ‡	12/2
330	1 July 1897	Landau	A	
90	17 March 1899	Charabanc	A ‡	20/4
316	12 June 1899	Victoria	A	
426	12 June 1899	Landau	A	ex G. Webb
86 (2nd use)	23 March 1900	Coach	A ‡	22/4; C/Ch 1903
256	28 June 1900	Victoria	A	
27	29 March 1901	Charabanc	A ‡	26/4
166	29 March 1901	Charabanc	A ‡	24/4
170	7 May 1901	Wagonette	A ‡	14/2
211	8 April 1902	Double chair	C	
256	8 April 1902	Double chair	C	
224	13 June 1902	Barouche	A	
254	13 June 1902	Barouche	A	
9	14 March 1904	Wagonette	A ‡	6/1
226	20 June 1904	Landau	A	to J. Trowbridge 1915
32	17 May 1904	Landau	A	
42	18 March 1907	Coach/charabanc	A ‡	17/4; Ch 1909
23 (3rd use)	18 March 1908	Wagonette	B ‡	5/1
52	17 March 1909	Charabanc	A ‡	23/4
24	18 April 1910	Charabanc	A	?/2
222	22 June 1910	Landau	A	

Thomas Elliott died 28 January 1911, aged 53, after which J. T. G. Elliott and W. E. Elliott ran the following vehicles: Nos 19 (charabanc), 21 (coach), 23 (brake), 24 (charabanc), 26 (coach), 42 (rebuilt as a normal charabanc), 86 (coach/charabanc) and 90 (charabanc), all licensed from 20 March 1911.

‡ Vehicles marked thus were licensed in a separate A-C series for what the council termed 'omnibuses' and referred to the work these licensed larger carriages were permitted to undertake. Vehicles not so marked were considered to be hackney carriages or 'cabs'; A = four-passenger capacity, B two-passenger, etc. In the case of 'omnibuses', 12/2 indicates a vehicle seating 12 passengers and drawn by two horses, etc.

* Capacity of all three of Tom Elliott's coaches was officially reduced to 22/4 by 3 May 1901, although only No 21 had its seating reduced, by two seats on top.

As described in *Glory Days: Royal Blue* (2000), following the death of his father in 1863 six-year-old Tom Elliott was sent to live with his uncle and aunt in Bournemouth. Aside from being a fishmonger Uncle George Cutler was the proprietor of a few bath chairs — small three-wheeled carriages, one-man-pulled along the flatter reaches of the emergent seaside resort. These conveyances featured a framed-glass suntrap of a door which closed over the lower half of the single passenger — usually an irritable female — who was invariably a recuperating patient from one of the numerous sanatoria for which the resort of Bournemouth was at that time unhappily famous. After Cutler progressed to handling pony-drawn bath chairs he probably found that served to redirect the more irascible comments toward the shambling quadruped. The largest and best-known of these convalescent homes was in the then appropriately named Sanatorium Road, which extended from the north-west corner of The Square to the Hotel Monte Dore and the sanitorium itself.

When, at the age of 22, in 1880, Thomas Elliott first acquired a licence to drive one of his uncle's horse-drawn 'double chairs' (two seats plus a driver) his allotted cab stand tended to be the one in Sanitorium Road. The Bournemouth Horse Committee minutes of 16 June 1882 noted that all was not as had been expected and that 'the conduct of drivers at the Sanatorium Road stand had been very objectionable, especially as regards the race and fight which had taken place there this week'. It was most likely in order to avoid such confrontations that Thomas Elliott was seen to be 'loitering about off the stand' with his cab 11 days later 'contrary to the provisions of the Bye-Laws'. The retribution meted out seems disproportionate in the light of such goings-on: his licence was suspended until 26 September 1883. In the interim his uncle had to take up the reins again. It was from this low-point in his young career that Thomas Elliott set out to establish himself as the best four-in-hand coach driver and proprietor in Bournemouth.

At the close of the 1883 season George Cutler possessed three double-chairs, a brougham and a landau — the latter pair four-seaters. Whilst the two-seaters became popular with those pleasantly disposed toward each other, the four-seaters proved ideal family-movers twixt hotel and railway stations. Well before he himself owned a carriage these, then, were the vehicles (and horses) with which the young Tom became soundly familiar.

Thomas Elliott acquired his first licence for a vehicle registered in his own name — a four-seat landau — on 8 October 1885, but his career as a proprietor did not take off until after the death of his uncle, in 1886. By 17 August 1888 he had become a competent four-in-hand driver (the reins of all four horses drawing a single carriage in the

hands of the driver), for on that date the Horse Committee took upon itself the right to issue licences for what it called 'omnibuses' to 10 local proprietors. Elliott received just one (No 23), for a 19-seat char-a-banc. The 23 vehicles licensed on that first day were nine 'proper' omnibuses, one wagonette, 10 chars-a-bancs and three brakes — and no 'stage coaches', of any stripe! Noteworthy, however is that only three proprietors' vehicles — all charabancs — were licensed at that time to be hauled by four horses: George Ames (two), Henry Laidlaw (one) and Elliott (one); he was among the elite. It seems highly likely that Elliott's 'No 23' — the first of his vehicles larger than a four-seat cab — was the first to be labelled 'Royal Blue', but the date of its acquisition is unknown.

During this period daily excursions as far afield as the New Forest, Wimborne and Lulworth Cove were made during the summer months only, because the carriages were permanently open. In inclement weather, therefore, the only passenger vehicles heading east out of Bournemouth were — so far as the records show — some of those other operators' omnibuses.

As several of the carriage proprietors turned increasingly toward larger vehicles drawn by two or more horses. so they adopted 'fleetnames'. Curiously Henry Laidlaw, who had the largest 'fleet' (five vehicles) when Bournemouth first issued licenses for 'omnibuses' in 1888, instead named his individually. Others may have done likewise. Hence this two-horse, 12-seat brake, 'The Star' (licence No 19), is merely 'likely' to have been his. At this time Thomas Elliott had just one (No 23), a four-horse, 19-seat charabanc.
Colin Morris collection

Right: In April 1892 Henry Laidlaw placed in service the first of the famous replica stage coaches, which competed for excursion passengers from stands in the vicinity of The Square for some 22 years thereafter. The following year he had two, as did Edward Lower; whilst G. R. Melton, of Lansdowne Stables, entered the fray with this 'Tally-Ho' replica coach, licensed to carry 24 passengers. It was to prove his only vehicle of its type — although his firm survived to run motor vehicles.
Colin Morris collection

Right: Thomas Elliott's first replica stage coach entered service in April 1894. A four-horse 24-seater, it was granted Bournemouth's Horse Committee Licence No 21. Belatedly concerned about the stability of such vehicles, the committee in 1901 reduced to 22 the number of passengers permissible for this type. By this time Elliott had just three such replicas. A much-modified 17-seater was added to his fleet in 1907; the maximum number of vehicles of this pattern he ever possessed, therefore, was four!
WNOC / Andrew Waller collection

The teams of four horses which hauled Tom Elliott's four replica stage coaches — the first of which (Licence No 21) entered service in April 1894 — although severely tried by pulling heavy loads along undulating roads, now had 'modern aids' to help them. Whereas in 'proper stage-coach days' the downhill momentum had to be held in check solely by the wheelers' (those two horses nearer the coach) digging in their heels and struggling to hold some two tons of vehicle, passengers and luggage, the 'replicas' of the late 19th century now had heavy-duty fore-and-aft driver-activated brakes upon the rear wheels. Although much of the work done by four-in-hand carriages took place in the 'spring-summer-autumn' season, a mild winter frequently saw them employed upon 'hot-punch and tinsel' trips from inn to inn around the New Forest and elsewhere. In the late part of the century the local Bournemouth newspapers had the potentially embarrassing habit of publishing the names of visitors to each hotel. That may be the reason that in one or two of the traditional 'departure photographs' which provided a good source of income for the local 'snapper', youngish couples may be seen attempting to hide behind such a news-sheet.

The Elliott brothers inherited their father's business and stock-in-trade in 1911 and in October 1912 began to replace the horse-drawn cabs — with a pair of Unic motor taxicabs operating initially from Bournemouth's railway stations; the first two motor charabancs arrived in March 1913. There was at that time no sign that, following World War 1 (1914-18), they would quickly outstrip their local rivals in that field. At one stage during the war those vehicles that had survived military requisition were licensed solely for the carriage of wounded servicemen.

Thereafter, despite the high quality of their competitors' vehicles, itineraries and personnel, the Elliott brothers began to display a winning mixture of successful risk-purchasing, quality of service and good all-round organisational skills and — in the early days, until local legislation stopped them — vigorous touting for custom at the roadside stands, particularly at the traditional departure-points in The Square, where John (Jack) Elliott's natural charm with the ladies

Right: Rival. This dark-red 18-seater Dennis charabanc, new in March 1913, was the second vehicle to carry the registration number EL 229. It entered service just five days before the Elliotts' first two motor charabancs (also of Dennis manufacture), but at 35hp was 7hp more powerful than its Royal Blue rivals. The vehicle was operated by Ernest and William Briant — 'Mark Briant's Executors'. The latter had been a contemporary of Thomas Elliott but had begun as a 'donkey boy' at the Pier and had run motor taxi-cabs from January 1909. *Alan Lambert collection*

Right: The Elliott brothers (Jack and Ted) purchased their first motor charabancs — a pair of Dennises with 20-seat Metcalfe bodywork — in March 1913. The chassis of both — and some Daimlers that followed — were requisitioned in World War 1. The bodies from the Dennises were refitted to the first of 15 American-built Selden chassis transhipped from the USA. They were very much a stopgap, being wooden-wheeled and of left-hand-drive configuration. This was EL 2626, new in May 1915. *Alan Lambert collection*

came in handy. A comprehensive series of excursions and longer tours was established which fanned out from Bournemouth, including a circular tour of the Isle of Wight at two guineas (£2.10) per head. For that the coaches were towed across the Solent in barges between Lymington and Yarmouth. Having acquired a surplus munitions works at Rutland Road in Bournemouth, which they converted into a garage and workshops, they used the parts left over to construct a garage at Yarmouth in 1922, thus dispensing with the need for barges and, at the same time, killing off a short-lived arrangement whereby Hants & Dorset ran passengers between Bournemouth and Lymington — and the Yarmouth (IW) Touring Co Ltd's violet-coloured charabancs made the circuit of the Island.

Left: 'Well-oiled by moonlight'. Informed that railways were to be built throughout the land, the Duke of Wellington remarked: "No good will come of it: that will allow the lower orders to move about!" What he would have thought about 27 lads of several ages singing and laughing aboard an open charabanc on a pub-crawl must be left to the imagination. EL 2001 was Elliott Bros' first Daimler to be powered by a 45hp 'Silent Knight' engine, noted for its quiet running — and heavy use of oil. Fitted with a locally built Ransom & Whitehead body, this vehicle entered service in June 1914, but in November 1917 the chassis was requisitioned for war service. *Colin Morris*

Left: Part of a Dalton's of Bournemouth private hire party-outing to the Cheddar Gorge and Caves, on 10 June 1920, is No 2B (EL 3837), a 30hp Daimler Y of 1919. The vehicle was of large capacity, being fitted with 29-seat Ransom & Whitehead bodywork featuring same-size acetylene head and side lamps. Despite its comparatively large-capacity engine this halt, in the Mendip Hills, may, judging by the open bonnet, have been a precautionary one — nothing too serious, however, for the general air of frivolity among the trippers appears undiminished. *Andrew Waller collection*

Left: Bearing a latter-day example of the 28-seater version of the locally built Ransom & Whitehead charabanc bodywork (if it still carried a step-ladder it was still a charabanc rather than a two-door coach) is No 2E (EL 6604) of 1922. This was one of the last Daimler Y-type vehicles delivered new to Royal Blue fitted with solid tyres, acetylene headlamps and oil side lights. However, it seems to have been a very reliable workhorse, for No 2E features in several pictures of the period taken beside the Upper Pleasure Gardens in Bournemouth. *Alan Lambert collection*

Above and right: Rival. Founded upon a Bournemouth-based carriage company dating from 1888, William Whitelock's firm became motorised in April 1913 with a blue-and-red Napier charabanc. A 32hp Commer in 'lavender' arrived in 1914, and a 40hp Thornycroft, painted grey, in 1919. Whitelock seems then to have sent Jas Bartle & Co of Notting Hill a photograph of a Ransom & Whitehead-bodied charabanc and said 'I'd like one like that', for this Leyland N (EL 4534) of 1920, with a rather angular Bartle version, turned up fitted (also by Bartle) with 'our Standard Hind Luggage Locker'. *Peter Delaney collection*

TELEPHONE 2628

TELEPHONE 2628

WHITE LOCK'S MOTOR COACH TOURS

By the Shamrock Motor Coaches, including the famous Leyland and Thornycroft Cars.

This Fleet consists of the most modern and up-to-date Cars in the District driven by reliable and experienced Chauffeurs.

Leaves the Square daily for all Places of Interest at popular fares.

Any of these Cars can be engaged privately for any tour or any distance on application to the

HEAD OFFICE: COTLANDS RD., or OXFORD RD. TAXIS & LUXURIOUS PRIVATE CARS FOR HIRE.

Although not the first to do so, the Elliott brothers re-wheeled and fitted pneumatic tyres to their fleet in time for the 1923 season. They had already provided a series of runs to London, having seized the opportunity to rescue passengers stranded in both Bournemouth and the capital by a National Union of Railwaymen's withdrawal of labour in 1919. Although the strike had been brief, much had been learned, and the following year Royal Blue charabancs began running to London on Fridays and Saturdays and returning each Saturday and Monday — not a particularly remunerative way of operating, but 1920 had seen the foundation established for the future Royal Blue Automobile Services network. It was at this time that an office and garage was acquired in Holdenhurst Road, Bournemouth, to develop this arm of the business.

Meanwhile, long-distance seven-day tours as far afield as Cornwall, Wales, the Lake District and Scotland were established, initially upon solid tyres, and these became even more popular after the fitting of pneumatics. In 1923, having made a show of preparing to run a series of stage-carriage services in the Bournemouth area, the Elliott bothers sold the 12 vehicles concerned to Hants & Dorset, which, in return, promised not to run coach tours, excursions or private-hire trips for the next 21 years. By this means they astutely shackled a serious potential competitor, although, as will be seen, events just 12 years later would render that arrangement null and void.

Above: Much depended upon the weather in the heyday of the open charabanc. In rain the raised 'cape-cart' hood did little to protect the passengers on the windward side. Fortunately the rain clouds have moved inland in time for this 1922 afternoon tour to go ahead as planned. About to depart from the lower end of Avenue Road, Bournemouth, is Daimler CK No 4A (EL 3736) of 1919. Its 18-seat bodywork, built locally, had probably been transferred from one of the short-lived Selden chassis.
Kithead Trust / Colin Morris

Above right: Rival. A. T. E Ransom's first motor charabanc was a Leyland 40hp model of 1912 — in other words, he actually began with mechanised transport before Elliott Bros. The vehicle featured in this advertisement is a 29-seat Ransom & Whitehead-bodied Leyland RAF-type 40hp model (EL 4689) of 1920 and, as stated, bore his fleet colour of 'chamois'. Ransom was at that time also proprietor of R&W Coachbuilders. In April 1924 he was to join forces with W. J. Whitelock to form Shamrock & Rambler Motor Coaches Ltd, based at 77 Holdenhurst Road, Bournemouth. *Colin Morris collection*

Left: Although Elliott Bros was not, as claimed, the first Bournemouth-based firm to fit its charabancs with pneumatic tyres, the commencement of the 1923 season for local tours saw much of the Royal Blue fleet proudly proclaiming that 'Pneumatic tyres mean Comfort'. Among them was No 1D (EL 5857), a Daimler Y-type 29-seater of 1921, parked two years later on the Lower Pleasure Gardens stand, collecting holidaymakers for a trip to Milford-on-Sea and the New Forest. The bodywork appears to have been built by Elliott Bros' own workforce. *Pamlin Prints*

Below: The fitting of pneumatic tyres not only provided a more comfortable ride; it also gave open charabancs a more substantial appearance. In addition the new cast wheels designed specially for them helped reduce the overall weight of each vehicle by some 5cwt. A case in point was this AEC YC 45hp charabanc of 1919 (with bodywork probably built by Royal Blue), No 7 (EL 3604), photographed on an excursion in 1926. The sky-blue livery has been enhanced by the addition of white waistband and bonnet-top, together with the ornate red-and-blue logo displayed until 1928, when overall royal blue was re-adopted as the fleet livery. *Colin Morris collection*

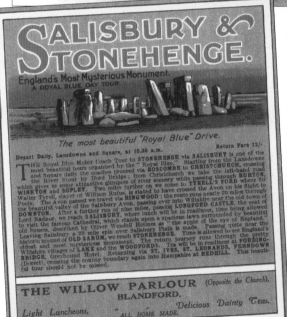

An apparent large gap in the new-vehicle intake between 1923 and 1928 is explained by the sheer durability of the Daimler CK and Y chassis already in stock. Concurrent with the fitting of pneumatic tyres, much of the locally-built bodywork was replaced with quadruple-purpose coachwork by London Lorries Ltd in an on-going programme of upgrading rather than scrapping existing vehicles. Elliott Bros had, in the meantime, concentrated its 'regular service' efforts upon the Bournemouth–London roads, becoming a member of the London Coastal Coaches organisation in 1925. Three summers later the Elliotts decided to market themselves as 'Royal Blue Automobile Services' — a decidedly transatlantic title.

At the London end the Elliotts' vehicles parked, like those of other operators at that time, in streets as near as possible to their booking offices. Then, in 1928, London Coastal Coaches succeeded in securing a makeshift parking lot in Lupus Street, near Vauxhall Bridge, and this served as an overcrowded terminus until the opening of Victoria Coach Station in 1932. It was whilst based at Lupus Street, however, that RBAS began its campaign to become a provider of wide-ranging express services. A London–Salisbury–Yeovil– Exeter–Plymouth route was started (to the consternation of Western National), together with another which joined forces with the pioneer Greyhound to link London, Reading, Bath, Bristol and Weston-super-Mare.

Left: Rival. New in 1920 as a solid-tyred charabanc, this Dennis 4-tonner underwent a significant makeover in 1924, when it was re-styled by London Lorries as a 21-seat two-door coach powered by an AEC engine. No 4 (EL 4814) of Symes & Sons Enterprise Motor Coaches was based in Tregonwell Road, Bournemouth. Enterprise (which name was usually a clue that an undertaking's first vehicles were Dennises) had a booking office at Malmesbury & Parsons' Dairy in The Square. The firm was to survive until acquired by Hants & Dorset in August 1938. *Ian Allan Library*

Below: In addition to updating its more sprightly charabancs by fitting them with new wheels and pneumatic tyres, Elliott Bros sent many Daimler Y and CK types to London Lorries Ltd, which firm turned them into two-doored coaches with staggered access to all seats and 'quadruple-purpose' all-weather bodies, along with its trademark V-shaped windscreen. Originally painted pale blue with a white stripe, they gained dark-blue upperworks and wings — and by 1928 had become 'royal blue' overall, which actually made them look smaller! *Colin Morris collection*

Left: Followed by a rather more modern Southdown Leyland Tiger bound for Portsmouth, a Royal Blue ADC 424 of 1928 departs the completely open yard which constituted the London Coastal Coaches Departure Station in Lupus Street, near Vauxhall Bridge, used from 1928 until the opening of Victoria Coach Station in 1932. The vehicle is one of just five Royal Blue ADC 424s bodied by Hall Lewis (the forerunner of Park Royal); all the others of this 1928 batch of 26 were built to a similar pattern by Duple. *Colin Morris collection*

In 1929 RBAS commenced running from Holdenhurst Road, Bournemouth, to Weston-super- Mare, to Dorchester, Exeter and Plymouth, to Yeovil, Taunton and Ilfracombe and — to the dismay of Southdown and East Kent — from Bournemouth right along the South Coast to Margate. The bold throw of 1929, however, was the long-striding northward thrust from Bournemouth to Salisbury, Swindon, Gloucester, Cheltenham and Birmingham. Realising the importance of Salisbury as the hub of the central-southern section of this expansion (no fewer than six roads into that city being now used by Royal Blue services), Jack Elliott took care to forge a special relationship with Raymond Longman of Wilts & Dorset Motor Services Ltd. On 26 June 1929, for instance, he was invited to address the W&D board, which resolved 'to make efforts to retain Elliott Bros' agency'. From that date Wilts & Dorset vehicles were readily made available as 'relief cars' to Royal Blue when called upon on summer weekends.

During this period of expansion separate licences for every coach had to be obtained from each local authority through which it would pass *en route*. Each came with an enamel plate, which had to be affixed to the rear of the vehicle. To ensure success in each locale Elliott Bros astutely employed former Police inspector Coole, who displayed a singular knack of leaving each Hackney Carriage Office armed with the necessary licence.

Meanwhile Jack Elliott drove himself and his staff to the limits of endurance. In what nowadays would be seen as positively dangerous, drivers were frequently worked to the point of exhaustion. Eric L. Jones recalled being asked to 'pop off to Plymouth' after returning from a round-trip from Bournemouth to London, resulting in an unexpected 27-hour shift — and that was, according to him, not unusual. Clement Preece (of whom more anon) joined RBAS as Publicity Manager in late 1929. He recalled (1974) 'Mr J.' (as he dubbed him) as 'a big man in many ways', with whom he had many 'rows', but that 'I remained loyal to him, and he to me'. The tours drivers, at least, got the better of him, 'on one memorable occasion dropping him over the railings of the gardens in The Square to cool off

after a particularly violent scene'. Preece opined that 'Mr J.' knew that no-one could tell him much about running the business. Harry Elliott he described as 'the financial brain behind the company [who] kept a strong rein on his more impetuous brother'.

The Road Traffic Act 1930 put an end to all the enamel plates. 'Mr J.' is credited with realising the need for a top legal team to fight Royal Blue's battles in the new traffic courts and successfully briefed Mr Walter Monckton and Mr Norman Fox-Andrews to do just that — as the subsequent grants of licences issued (which appeared in the 'Notices & Proceedings published by the Traffic Commissioners) duly showed.

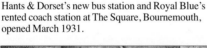

Hants & Dorset's new bus station and Royal Blue's rented coach station at The Square, Bournemouth, opened March 1931.

By the late 1920s both the Bournemouth council and operators of stage-carriage services and coach tours were anxious about the overcrowding of roadside stands, particularly around The Square. The generally good relationship between Hants & Dorset Motor Services Ltd and Elliott Bros now relieved the problem considerably. A joint omnibus and coach station was built on the south side of The Square, where a small hill, between there and the seafront, had aided the construction of an ingenious two-tier structure. Hants & Dorset buses in effect went 'upstairs', while Royal Blue coaches dived into the depths beneath — 'down the chute', as the drivers called it. The station opened on Sunday 8 March 1931.

Only Royal Blue's express services (and those of its associated express providers) used the station, the vehicles entering via 'the chute' on the right, proceeding anti-clockwise around a central waiting hall and luggage room, exchanging their passengers and exiting by means of the ramp on the left as viewed from The Square (until a major enlargement of the building in 1958). At night the station was a blaze of light, the names of the two operators — and a clock on the façade — being illuminated in red.

As built, the coach station provided for 10 coaches to park and six to load at the same time, while passengers came and went through two openings into Exeter Lane, on the east side, or used the staircase to the upper (Hants & Dorset) level. When the coach station was full in summer an electric exhaust-extractor was brought into action. There were two petrol pumps in the coach station, one in each corner. A correspondent with *Bus & Coach* in April 1931 noted that 'the building is practically fire-proof … if one sprinkler is opened by the heat of a fire it will cause the fire-alarm to sound' — and indeed 'fireproof' it remained until that fateful night 45 years later, when just such a fire in the extended part of the coach station caused the abandonment of the entire structure.

At the time of the station's opening in 1931 there were 18 express arrivals and departures daily, including seven for London each day in winter and, in the summer, 23, with considerable duplication. The luggage was stored according to routes with different-coloured tickets for each and which corresponded with appropriate Royal Blue advertising, handbills and posters. Elliott Bros called the conductors on its express coaches 'inspectors'; one was allocated to each service, and he was responsible for all 'relief cars' duplicating that service. Each 'inspector' was answerable to the station superintendent. All charting from sub-agents and offices was carried out in a special office at the station.

In 1934 Royal Blue Automobile Services was one of six operators which joined forces to form 'Associated Motorways', based upon Black & White Motorways' headquarters at Cheltenham; the other participant companies were Greyhound Motor Services, Midland Red, Red & White and United Counties. Revenue was allotted upon a mileage basis, to the economic benefit of the association's members. It incidentally meant that coaches in Royal Blue livery began to appear in pastures completely new, for each company still retained its own colours, and only the association's publicity material depicted a 'neutral' coach in garish orange and green.

The newly built Omnibus & Coach Station on the south side of The Square, Bournemouth. The light atop the left-hand pole was green, representing Hants & Dorset buses, while that on the right was blue, for Royal Blue Automobile Services. The former went up the ramp, keeping to the left, and went around clockwise to emerge beneath the word 'STATION'. Royal Blue coaches put their tails in the air, heading 'down the chute' to the right of the ramp, and went 'downstairs' and around anti-clockwise, to emerge, re-loaded, to the left of the ramp.
Colin Morris collection

Harry Rollings had joined Royal Blue in 1922 and soon found himself dealing with a great deal of the paperwork. In the early days this was done under the supervision of Harry Elliott. Found to be up to the mark, Rollings was given the title General Manager, being nominally responsible for the day-to-day running of the company — although Jack Elliott from time to time decided that he himself also was General Manager. Then, in 1929, Clement Preece, who had been invited to a meeting about a new-fangled heating system, was instead offered a new post — that of Publicity Manager. Clearly Harry Elliott, officially the firm's Secretary, had recognised in Preece a distinct flair for communication.

Thus it was that when the traffic courts began to function in 1931 and Royal Blue's high-powered legal team was first briefed, 'Mr J.' had the good sense to see that what was needed in court was a regular cool-headed witness to answer questions both friendly and hostile to the cause — in short, someone to impress the Traffic Commissioners. Preece promptly became Elliotts' Traffic Manager. The coaching world had changed. Whereas, previously, numerous operators had run the opposition off the road, in future applications granted or refused would be decided in court before a wheel was turned. Passengers and drivers were about to enjoy a new and safer era. The Elliott brothers appointed Preece to be their regular court witness and principal representative. An early case brought by Southdown and East Kent (and backed by the Southern Railway) found the Elliotts defending their right to continue running their express service between Bournemouth and Margate. The outcome had been an equitable arrangement whereby it was divided into three parts — Bournemouth–Portsmouth, Portsmouth–Hastings and Hastings–Margate. Each company was to share in the through-running, and the proceeds would be divided equally. Mr J.'s presence was required simply to sign the agreement.

Mr Royal Blue' — Clement Preece — demonstrating that inimitable traffic courtroom stare which served to represent either incredulity or astonishment. Whichever, it frequently appeared to help identify a flaw in the case being put for an operational opponent. More often than not, Royal Blue walked away with the licences the joint Southern and Western National companies really wanted. *C. H. Preece / Colin Morris*

Rival. By the time this poster was issued, in 1930, Clement Preece was working for Elliott Bros at Bournemouth. However, between 1927 and 1929 Preece had been manager — and general factotum — for Modern Travel Ltd (previously Kingston & Modern Travel Ltd) at Southampton. Its coaches were financed by hire purchase companies and were generally overpowered and difficult to maintain. This Lycoming TS-engined Gifford 166OT coach (TR 8061) with 28-seat Wycombe coachwork entered service with Modern Travel in January 1930 and was the company's penultimate vehicle. *Colin Morris collection*

There followed proceedings head to head with Greyhound, Devon General and Midland Red, among others. Royal Blue's contribution to the history of such matters was crystallised in *Notices & Proceedings* as the 'Elliott Summation of Fares Appeal Precedent'. Clem Preece's fascinating autobiography *Wheels to the West* (1974) covers these events in some detail, and the articulate wit of the man makes it a very good read. To quote just one example, in describing a very serious altercation in court he writes: 'The atmosphere was tense — even the dead flies on the window sill seemed to wake up!'

In a quiet way the year 1933 was quite important. As described in *Southern National Omnibus Company* (2007), the National Omnibus & Transport holding company's 'London & Coastal Business' based at Shepherd's Bush, as extant, was dissolved, Eastern, Southern and Western National assuming control of the appropriate parts of its coaching activity in London from a joint booking office at 206 Brompton Road. By 1928 National's 'London & Coastal' had established five express routes from London to points in the West Country — Weymouth, Bude, Ilfracombe, Newquay and Penzance. After their formation in 1929, the responsibility for running these services passed to Southern National (the first three) and Western National — although, as far as stage-carriage services were concerned, Newquay was officially in Southern National territory. Both firms, with the backing of the Southern Railway and the GWR respectively, were now firmly committed to the running of long-distance express work. It may seem surprising that railway representatives on the board of each should concur over the perceived need for such activity upon the roads, but if any road service of that kind were to be established it was, in their view, far better that they should be able to have a say as to how it should be run.

Accordingly, in April 1933, both SNOC and WNOC full boards heard that an approach with a view to purchase had been made to Elliott Bros (Bournemouth) Ltd, which had responded by sending to their joint headquarters copies of its audited accounts for the year to 30 September 1932. That year also it had been the joint purchase by SNOC and WNOC of the express services operated hitherto by Highways (1933) Ltd and Highways (Bournemouth) Ltd that gave public notice of their intent. A 'working agreement' with Elliott Bros had been established by the end of 1933.

Then, one fine day in November 1934, Clement Preece's office at Royal Blue headquarters in Holdenhurst Road was invaded by several smiling directors of Thomas Tilling Ltd and of the Southern and

Western National companies. For long part of the 'opposition' in so many Traffic Court hearings, they now wanted him to do something similar for them. With effect from 1 January 1935 the 'Royal Blue' brand became the property of the Thomas Tilling organisation.

As Bournemouth was the location of the headquarters of its stage-carriage subsidiary, Hants & Dorset Motor Services Ltd, Tilling decided that because the latter firm was thus now released from its pledge (of 1924) not to run tours, excursions or private hires, Hants & Dorset should be permitted to purchase that aspect of the Elliott brothers' business — and that Southern and Western National should jointly acquire the express-service workings. Accordingly the Elliott fleet was split three ways, giving Harry Rollings, already earmarked to become Tours Manager for Hants & Dorset, the opportunity to choose which vehicles in particular should go with him to his new employer. Not surprisingly he made sure that Hants & Dorset acquired all four of the Elliott brothers' most recent coaches — the revolutionary full-fronted, underfloor- and amidships-engined AEC Q-type vehicles, which Preece described as 'sensational'; 'they rode like a Rolls-Royce, and people literally asked to travel on them'.

Despite the fact that Southern and Western National gained title to the Royal Blue name in 1935 by purchasing the express business previously run by Elliott Bros (Bournemouth) Ltd, the parent National company actually had motor buses undertaking excursion work at least a season before the Elliotts became motorised. Pictured in 1914, these five Clarkson double-deckers of the National Steam Car Co Ltd, led by F 6160 (No 91) and F 5213 (No 57) — both of 1912 — of Shepherd's Bush depot, are taking a break from duty on route 12 to run an excursion. A classic hansom cab rumbles by. *Alan Lambert collection*

Right: The first AEC Q chassis to be fitted with a coach body has turned up at AEC headquarters at Southall, Middlesex, for a celebratory photo-call in July 1933. The vehicle, LJ 8001, completed by Duple, was a 35-seater built for Elliott Bros (Bournemouth) Ltd — the first of four such chassis purchased for Royal Blue. Upon acquisition of the firm by Tillings the quartet was snapped up by Hants & Dorset Motor Services Ltd. *Ian Allan Library*

Right: The fourth and final AEC Q coach purchased by Elliott Bros, in 1934, was a 35-seater bodied by Harrington, of Hove, Sussex, with observation-style floor slope and split waistline — a configuration that was to become popular in the late 1930s. AEL 2 (later Hants & Dorset's No Q446) was photographed outside the Pavilion Garage, Bath Road, bearing H&D legal lettering but retaining the royal-and-sky-blue livery of Elliott Bros. *Colin Morris collection*

Left: Royal Blue AEC Qs LJ 8600 of November 1933 and AEL 2 of June 1934 head a line-up of touring coaches ranged across the entrance to the Lower Pleasure Gardens in Bournemouth. In this classic period piece a tram still provides the shuttle service up Richmond Hill, two Sunbeam trolleybuses and a DuCros saloon head west, and an AEC double-decker prepares to circumnavigate the central passenger-pens, all five of these vehicles being in the service of Bournemouth Corporation.
Colin Morris collection

Below: Most of Elliott Bros' existing Royal Blue Automobile Services vehicles were simply re-labelled with SNOC/WNOC's version of the Royal Blue fleetname (which between the words incorporated a winged wheel and 'cloud of dust' logo) and continued to visit their old haunts with ex-Elliott crews. SNOC's No 3731 (LJ 1525), an AEC Regal/Duple 28-seater of 1930, was pictured at Digbeth in 1935, with a Birmingham Corporation trolleybus in the background. The Plymouth–Birmingham service had been run by Royal Blue on behalf of Associated Motorways since the previous year. *The Omnibus Society*

Southern and Western National took over the lease (from Hants & Dorset) of the lower-floor coach station at Bournemouth, and this became the centre of control and charting for their now greatly enlarged series of express coach operations. In addition both firms now inherited membership of the Associated Motorways organisation (on whose behalf Clement Preece had also been active). Very sensibly, SNOC/WNOC also decided to put all their express-service work, new and old, under the Royal Blue name, and to retain the dark-blue livery — probably one of the simplest but most astute marketing decisions ever made in the coaching industry.

With his new firm Clement Preece was transferred from Bournemouth to SNOC/WNOC headquarters in Exeter, where he was redesignated Traffic Superintendent (Express Services). Such was the responsibility which would become attached to this role, it was here that he earned the soubriquet 'Mr Royal Blue'.

At the same time Thomas Tilling made a similar purchase of the rather smaller firm of Tourist Coaches (Southampton) Ltd — and in the same manner divided the assets and vehicles three ways between SNOC/WNOC and Hants & Dorset, the major operator locally, thus

Above: New to Tourist Coaches (Southampton) Ltd as No 42 (OW 1878) was this Albion Valiant PV70, pictured at the Strachans factory prior to delivery in July 1932. It became Western National No 3525 in May 1935 but did not join the Royal Blue fleet.
Alan Lambert collection

Right: Modern Travel Ltd was, in effect, run off the road by the competing 26-seat Strachans-bodied Albion and Leyland vehicles of Tourist Motor Coaches (Southampton) Ltd. Tourist had started in earnest in January 1921, when Bertie H. Ransom started tours from Southampton with two GMC 14-seat charabancs based in Back of the Walls. His firm became a limited-liability company in November 1927. Its logo, familiar locally until 1935, is here displayed on the rear of No 39 (TR 9920), a 20-seat Strachans-bodied Leyland Cub KP1 of 1931.
Colin Morris collection

giving the latter title to the 'Tourist' name for use on the coaches it would now operate from Southampton. Tourist had been founded by Bertie H. Ransom. He started express workings after running stranded ship's passengers to London during the General Strike of 1926. The firm had become Tourist Coaches (Southampton) Ltd in 1927 following an input from S. C. Bullock and Thomas Briggs. The firm then absorbed W. Aloysius Browne's Hiawatha Motor Coaches, which as 'Queen Motor Coaches' had actually pioneered express road travel from Southampton to London with a pair of 14-seat Crossley charabancs.

The revitalised Tourist had purchased Major James Jackson's Coliseum Coaches and employed him in a managerial role in the tours sector. On the express-services side the firm established three route variations, initially between Southampton and London (Embankment) but extending westward to Bournemouth in 1929. From the following year it went much farther west, to Exeter, Torquay and Plymouth, employing vehicles specially adapted with 'close-third' gears enabling them to tackle the notorious Telegraph Hill, south of Exeter.

On 1 June, however, and to provide a link for those connected with the shipping businesses in the two ports, Tourist introduced an express service with Leyland Tigers between Southampton and Liverpool, running via Winchester, Oxford, Stratford-upon-Avon — and within sight of the 'Ladies of the Vale' (the three spires of Lichfield Cathedral) — and Warrington, where connections were arranged with local operators for Bolton, Manchester and Wigan. This service ran three times a week and by 1933 had been extended at the southern end to Bournemouth, operating northbound on Sundays, Tuesdays and Thursdays and southbound from Liverpool on Mondays, Wednesdays and Fridays; during August it operated daily. Upon acquisition by Tilling the fleet was, as before, split three ways, Western National gaining 12 vehicles, and Southern National and Hants & Dorset 11 apiece.

The portfolio of express services was subsumed by SNOC/WNOC under the 'Royal Blue' title, which name thereafter appeared regularly on the north bank of the River Mersey. Hants & Dorset acquired the 'Tourist Coach Station' in Grosvenor Square, Southampton and title to 'Tourist, Southampton' which appeared on its coaches in the form of 'Royal Blue and Tourist', as displayed until 1947. Bertie H. Ransom, meanwhile, used some of his cash derived from the sale to buy shares in and become a director of Southampton Football & Athletic Club, based at The Dell, home of the 'Saints', in Archers Road. Of the Tourist vehicles which went to the National companies, most joined the green-and-cream fleets, only two Leyland Tigers and an AEC Regal serving at length in Royal Blue livery.

Above: Upon the reorganisation of Tourist in 1927 the company purchased Hiawatha Motor Coaches, of Winchester Road, Southampton. The premises had previously been the property of the Vivid Motor Touring Co. This Dennis 29-seat charabanc (CR 4575) of 1921 — pictured on Bath Hill, Bournemouth — had been part of that fleet, which passed into the hands of W. Aloysius Browne, of Copeswood Road, Bitterne Park, east of the River Itchen. Browne was at that time trading as 'Queen Motor Coaches'.
Alan Lambert collection

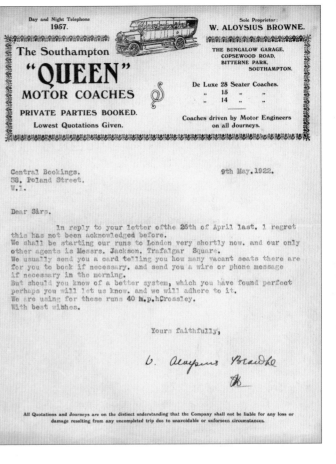

Left: This Crossley 25hp 14-seat charabanc (CR 6836) of 1922 was one of a pair purchased by W. A. Browne whilst trading as Queen Motor Coaches from his base in Bitterne Park. Both were used to provide a Southampton–London express service, some four years before B. H. Ransom's 'Tourist' charabancs ran to the capital during the General Strike of 1926 and six before the latter became a regular operator to the capital. When Browne bought Hiawatha the fleetnames were displayed either way around. *Alan Lambert collection*

Right: Rival. Also posed on Bath Hill whilst on a summer's-day trip from Southampton to Bournemouth is this 28-seat Maudslay charabanc (CR 5911) of 1921, wearing the primrose-yellow livery of Jock T. Cousin's 'The Richmond', of Foundry Lane, Freemantle, Southampton. From 1925 until 1927 Cousin was to engage with Hants & Dorset Motor Services Ltd in the 'Battle of Lyndhurst', using six Lancias and a specially tuned Leyland Lion PLSC1. After a fares war which saw hundreds enjoy 'give-away' prices to the New Forest from Southampton, Cousin capitulated on 28 November 1927. *Alan Lambert collection*

Right: Rival. At least 28 ladies and infants are packed aboard this 23-seater charabanc (OT 629) on a trip from Southampton to Lymington and the New Forest. This elegant vehicle was an REO with London Lorries coachwork, first registered on 31 March 1926. Named 'The Orchid', it was delivered to Tombs & Drake, of Totton, once dubbed the largest village in England; R. H. Tombs and James Drake were based at little Testwood Garage, The Causeway, and had another garage at Ower, on the road to Romsey. *Colin Morris collection*

Left: The livery adopted by Tourist Motor Coaches (Southampton) Ltd had been medium blue to the waistrail and bonnet-top, which were cream, and dark blue above. Albion PKB26/Strachans 26-seater No 25 (TR 6335) of 1929 demonstrates the arrangement, with simple lining-out in gold. Upon acquisition of Tourist by Tillings in 1935 the fleet was split three ways (as with Elliott Bros' fleet) between SNOC, WNOC and Hants & Dorset; this vehicle would become a green-and-cream coach as Southern National No 3532. *Pamlin Prints*

Below: When Thomas Tilling Ltd supervised the purchase of Elliott Bros (Bournemouth) Ltd's 'Royal Blue Automobile Services' it was agreed that the fleet should be split three ways between the participant subsidiary operators — Southern and Western National and Hants & Dorset. The last-named for two seasons retained much of the royal blue, painting the remainder of each vehicle turquoise in the manner depicted upon ex-Elliott Daimler CF6 No N418 (LJ 1501), one of five Duple-bodied examples acquired by H&D together with 10 ADC, nine AEC Reliance (unused), six AEC Regal and one Leyland Tiger TS2. *J. T. Wilson / Colin Morris*

Below: Upon acquisition of its share of Royal Blue vehicles in January 1935 Hants & Dorset continued to use the Royal Blue title but in deference to Southern/Western National, which had wisely decided to embrace the name for all of its newly enlarged express network, placed it discreetly on the flanks of its new touring, excursion and private-hire fleet within this impressive and tastefully designed garter. After acquisition of the Tourist firm similar vehicles bore 'TOURIST / SOUTHAMPTON' within the garter for two services; then, from 1937 to 1947, 'ROYAL BLUE and TOURIST' on green-and-cream coaches. *Colin Morris*

Right: In anticipation of its takeover of the allotted one-third share of the Royal Blue fleet (in order to undertake the tours and excursions business from Bournemouth in time for the 1935 season) Hants & Dorset arranged to have built a fleet of 14 new Leyland Tiger coaches bodied in a special streamlined style by J. C. Beadle, of Dartford. Ten were to be allocated to the Royal Blue fleet at Bournemouth and four to the 'Tourist' counterpart at Southampton. Both fleets were to be painted royal blue and turquoise.
Colin Morris collection

Right: The original design work for the bodywork chosen for Hants & Dorset for its new fleet of streamlined coaches was carried out by Brush, at Loughborough. It would appear, however, that, due to a heavy workload, Brush was unable to proceed with the work on the prototype, and the 14 delivered in 1935 had been sub-contracted to Beadle. To Brush's dismay Beadle subtly improved the design, yet months later, when the Loughborough-built example — No F536 (BLJ 394) — finally arrived, the awkward lines of the original had been adhered to.
Colin Morris collection

The year 1935 saw the acquisition by Hants & Dorset of four local coach concerns; White Heather, Billies Coaches, Byways Ltd and Parma Violet Coaches. It seems likely that this one-off Thornycroft Lightning GC/SC6 with Wadham Coachwork, No S532 (BEL 607), delivered new to H&D in August 1935, had been on order for Parma Violet. It was posted to Southampton for use in the Tourist fleet, painted in the briefly 'standard' livery of royal blue and turquoise. *Colin Morris collection*

All three Tilling subsidiaries had laid plans for brand-new coaches to be built for them as soon as it became clear that the purchases of RBAS and Tourist were in the bag. Hants & Dorset chose Leyland Tigers, and because of Western National's connection with its then subsidiary, the Bristol Tramways & Carriage Co (together with its manufacturing arm), both SNOC and WNOC chose the Bristol JJW chassis as the base for their new 1935 Royal Blue fleet of 28 coaches divided equally between the two. A Mumford-influenced style of bodywork, to seat 32 passengers but built by Beadle, Eastern Counties and MCW, was chosen for this new fleet. With minor variations this style of bodywork was to remain in production for further Royal Blue coaches until the outbreak of World War 2 in 1939.

Apart from the touring coaches of Elliott Bros, Royal Blue express coaches had not served Cornwall, which duchy, as a result of the purchases, now found itself part of the greatly expanded Royal Blue network. Indeed, when four 'non-stop' services were started soon afterward, a 'Cornish Coast Express' to Penzance joined those dubbed 'Channel Coast Express' (to Bournemouth), 'Minehead Express' and 'Weymouth Bay Express'.

Clement Preece meanwhile had discovered that SNOC and WNOC had tended to believe that their original express services should be run at the weekends and primarily for summer visitors to the West Country. He proposed instead to introduce year-round schemes, with coaches making stops in all the towns and villages along the way.

Right: To cater for smaller touring parties Hants & Dorset in 1936 invested in three Leyland KPZ2 Cubs, for which Beadle scaled down its semi-observation style of bodywork. No L452 (CEL 223) bears the new 'ROYAL BLUE and TOURIST' title inside the H&D garter, and this was retained (until 1947) even though the blue-and-turquoise livery was replaced by cream and green in time for the start of the 1937 touring season. Two KPZ4 Cubs to a similar pattern would be added in 1939.
Colin Morris collection

Right: The paintshop at Hants & Dorset's Winchester Road depot went into overdrive during the close season of 1936/7. Whether by in-house decision or by Tilling diktat has not been recorded, but the livery for H&D's tours and excursion fleet lost its royal blue and turquoise, which were replaced by cream and Tilling green, with wings in BET dark green; 'ROYAL BLUE and TOURIST' was now reduced to a 9½in 'Solito' transfer within the H&D garter. Leyland Tiger TS7/Beadle No F564 (CEL 229) demonstrates.
Colin Morris collection

Left: As soon as negotiations for the purchase of Elliott Bros' Royal Blue Automobile Services became a certainty, in 1934, SNOC/WNOC ordered 28 Bristol JJW chassis to be fitted with 32-seat coachwork built to a common design by three firms — Eastern Counties (eight), Weymann and Beadle (10 each). They were divided equally between Southern and Western National. No 185 (ATT 935) was delivered to the former in 1935 painted in royal blue, turquoise and cream with hammered-aluminium bonnet. *Andrew Waller collection*

Left: Southern National purchased R. G. W. Austin's Greyhound Coaches (Weymouth) Ltd in January 1936, thus gaining express services for naval personnel travelling between Portland to either Plymouth or Portsmouth. It had previously acquired Austin's Saturdays-only express Weymouth–London service, in May 1934, prior to SNOC/WNOC's gaining title to Royal Blue. Among the 17 vehicles acquired by SNOC was this Dennis GL/Duple 20-seater of 1928, previously with Austin's Victory Motors (Weymouth) Ltd and which had been one of the inaugurating London express coaches in 1929. *Colin Morris collection*

Right: In November 1935 SNOC and WNOC began a process of rebodying selected ex-Elliott vehicles with new replacements built by Beadle and, in some cases, Duple. AEC Regal No 3627 (LJ 1511) received this 32-seat forward-entrance Beadle body in December of that year, becoming the first of its type to be thus upgraded. It was photographed in 1953 parked in Ebury Street, awaiting collection by the driver from nearby Victoria Coach Station, whence it would resume its function as a 'relief car' in the parlance of the period.
Andrew Waller collection

This would entail significant readjustment to the existing timetables, but from a remunerative angle it seemed the obvious thing to do. He met considerable opposition about this from within the joint companies, but once Bernard Venn Smith became General Manager of both, in January 1936, Preece received full backing for his plans. They were duly implemented and led to the engagement, at little cost, of numerous additional booking offices from elegant new premises right down to the little one-room tobacconist's and newspaper shop in a village terrace — like, for instance, Wally Bennett's at 13 East Street, Titchfield (Hants), where great excitement was occasioned by the periodic arrival of the Royal Blue van carrying copies of Preece's latest publicity material, but where, right there and then, one could nevertheless book a return trip to such exotic places as Penzance or Margate.

The fleetname and logotype for SNOC/WNOC's new Royal Blue coaches incorporated a winged wheel, bearing the individual company's name (Southern or Western National), which until after World War 2 trailed a small cloud of dust — very Wordsworthian: 'But trailing clouds of Glory do we come'.

Upon the outbreak of war in 1939 there was much scurrying back and forth with rather nervous evacuees (who feared an immediate

attack by hordes of Luftwaffe aircraft but found that didn't happen) and a more considered evacuation of schoolchildren from London and the larger centres of population, planned by Government and organised by the relative local authority. The cost of removing whole schools (plus some of the teachers) was funded by the former, and Royal Blue sprang into action on 31 August 1939 (just before war was actually declared), collecting hundreds of youngsters — some tearful and others excited, but all wearing name-tags in case they forgot who they were and carrying their gas-masks and little bags of belongings — from Victoria Coach Station, all for points west that they'd never seen before and, at first, didn't much like. Many other vehicles owned by the SNOC and WNOC companies were thrown into the fray to assist.

Left: Southern National's No 3721 (LJ 650) was a noteworthy vehicle in that it was the first of the comparative quartet of coaches purchased for evaluation purposes by Elliott Bros in 1929. It was thus the first AEC Regal chassis acquired for service with Royal Blue Automobile Services. This 31-seat forward-entrance body by Beadle replaced the Duple original in April 1937. The coach is pictured acting as a relief car on Royal Blue route E, London–Reading–Bath–Bristol (joint with Greyhound) — a six-hour journey, unless non-stop between London and Marlborough, as on Wednesdays and Saturdays in summer.
East Pennine Transport Group / Andrew Waller collection

Left: It says a great deal for the products of Leyland that three of the Tiger TS2 coaches which joined the Western National fleet in 1929 — having previously served with the parent company, the National Omnibus Transport Co Ltd — were deemed fit and spritely enough in 1937 to receive the appropriate new coachwork rendering them fit to join the ranks of Royal Blue. Like its two sisters, likewise upgraded, No 2863 (UU 1566) sported a 26-seat Beadle body and an upgraded 'Covrad' radiator embellished with 'ROYAL BLUE' and 'TIGER' badges.
Andrew Waller collection

Right: After requisition of the Royal Blue brand in 1935, both Southern and Western National had a considerable advantage in hand — vehicles already based in the West Country which could provide onward feeder services to destinations off the main express routes. Surely one of the more peculiar was this Dennis Mace with 20-seat coach body by Duple. The absence of the driver's awkward entrance door (under repair), together with its 'last-panel' passenger door, add to the quaint appearance of No 3760 (AYA 60), acquired in 1938 from S. T. Heard's Red Deer Coaches, of Minehead. *Andrew Waller collection*

There having been no serious attacks upon towns at the outset, adults and some children began to drift back, and Royal Blue obliged until, in the summer of 1940, the air-raid sirens began to wail in earnest. Heavy traffic to the West Country resumed, and Royal Blue was once again called upon to lend many experienced helping hands.

During this early period of uncertainty there were plenty of customers also for Royal Blue in the form of soldiers on weekend passes going back and forth from camps in Devon, Somerset, Dorset and on Salisbury Plain, in Wiltshire. On such journeys to London and elsewhere military personnel paid the conductor (as SNOC/WNOC now called them) aboard each coach and received a National ticket in exchange. Royal Blue lore has it that one conductor was suspected of pocketing the money and not issuing all with a ticket. One dark evening a uniformed inspector boarded his coach and travelled as far as the nearest military camp, where he waited as soldiers came aboard, then he said 'Good night' and stepped off into the gloom. The vehicle travelled several miles to the next camp, where more 'squaddies' boarded — followed by the very same inspector. He had 'ridden shotgun', clinging to the luggage ladder at the back of the coach. Royal Blue personnel didn't seem too concerned about what happened to the unfortunate conductor but, as ex-driver Howard Evans relates, 'proved anxious to know how that very dedicated inspector managed to hold on to his cap!'

When, from September 1940, Luftwaffe raids became very heavy, brave Royal Blue passengers and their even more heroic drivers kept going towards their destinations, frequently warned by an increasingly red glow in the sky miles ahead of what terrors awaited them. London, Plymouth, Southampton, Portsmouth, Bristol and later (in 1942) even mediæval Exeter were being heavily attacked. In at least one instance a Royal Blue coach was accelerated upon its way to the capital by a high-explosive bomb which landed immediately behind it — just one second slower and …! Passengers and driver aboard that coach were physically unhurt, but their ears whistled uncomfortably for days afterward. No 'counselling' in those days! Later Bournemouth Coach Station was damaged, and Victoria Coach Station was surrounded by

fire and high-explosive destruction but escaped relatively undamaged. However, several Royal Blue coaches parked nearby had windows and panelling broken by flying debris, but they went out on service the following morning patched up as best possible by their drivers and stalwart London-based Royal Blue staff.

The London–Southampton–Bournemouth route was kept going at half strength until the autumn of 1942. Bournemouth–Southampton–Portsmouth continued to operate (Luftwaffe permitting) in a similar manner, as did Bournemouth–Ilfracombe. Following tremendous damage to its city centre, routes to Plymouth were reduced in frequency by up to two-thirds — and most of the rest were simply discontinued for the remainder of the war. In the case of the latter, difficulties had arisen by the need to keep a large number of drivers on permanent standby against the possibility of invasion or other military requirements. Anderson & Frankis (1970) note that the Royal Blue fleet strength at this time was 91 coaches.

In October 1942 all express coach operation nationwide came to a standstill following a Government order to do so, principally to save fuel for the war effort. Clem Preece, however, succeeded in convincing the Ministry of War Transport and the Regional Transport Commissioners (as they were called in World War 2) that a limited number of Royal Blue coaches should be permitted to run upon six routes 'of national importance' for the use of munitions workers and

military personnel in areas which had been deprived of transport by the suspension of express services. These in the main were centred upon Bournemouth (for details of which see the accompanying map). The services in the event were set to operate for some 3½ years, save route 405, which kept going as a kind of stage-carriage service (intrusively so, thought Hants & Dorset) until 1949.

Several petrol-engined Royal Blue coaches removed from their usual duties as a result of the war were converted at Western National's Taunton depot to run on gas brewed up in an anthracite-burning trailer — for illustrations see *Southern National Omnibus Company* (2007). Examples of both SNOC and WNOC Bristol JJW coaches, 17 in all, were modified to tow the trailers, together with eight Western National Leyland Tigers. One or two of these vehicles

temporarily lost their Royal Blue identities, wearing a green and cream livery and being labelled 'Southern National' or 'Western National' accordingly. Examples in either blue or green were to be seen trundling along as far afield from Taunton as Bridport in Dorset and other areas not too strenuous. As with other vehicles converted in like manner nationwide, they proved sluggish and, on the South Coast, rather than helping the war effort, got in the way of swifter-moving military convoys — British, Canadian and, to a larger extent, in that part of the West Country, those of the United States of America. Following some well-aimed and thoroughly justified military invective they were discreetly removed from service and hidden away in various garages, never to be seen again — in that configuration, at least.

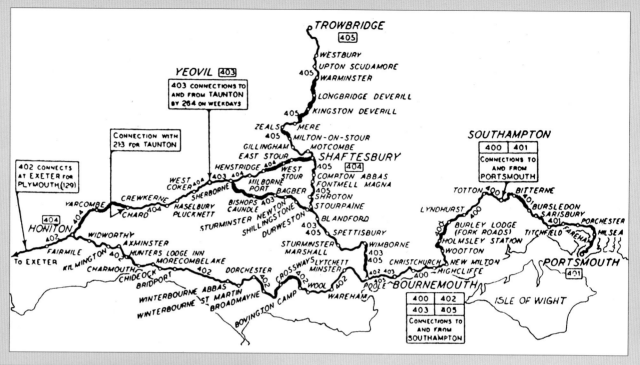

Below: In the dark days of World War 2 express services nationwide came to a halt, although some Royal Blue coaches were kept running on six routes 'of national importance'. Others towed gas-producing trailers, to save petrol, whilst Southern National's No 1065 (ETA 999) was painted green (where previously it was blue) and ran on stage-carriage services based upon Yeovil. It was photographed working on the roundabout country route (64) to Sherborne, Stalbridge and Shaftesbury whilst in full wartime rig of masked headlamps and white wingtips. *The Omnibus Society*

SER NO	VEH REQ	DURATION	JOURNEY	JOURNEYS EACH WAY
400	1	88 mins	Bournemouth–Southampton	4
401	1	62 mins	Southampton–Portsmouth	4
402	3	250 mins	Bournemouth–Dorchester–Bridport–Honiton–Exeter (interworked with SN service 47)	2
403	1	136 mins	Bournemouth–Blandford - Sherborne–Yeovil	1
404	1	167 mins	Honiton–Chard–Yeovil - Shaftesbury (one short each way Chard–Honiton)	1
405	2	215 mins	Bournemouth–Blandford–Shaftesbury–Warminster–Trowbridge	2

Six World War 2 routes of national importance centred upon Bournemouth. *Map and table courtesy Calton Phoenix*

Left: Following the outbreak of World War 2 in September 1939 all Hants & Dorset's tours and excursion work was suspended for the duration of hostilities. All 14 of Hants & Dorset's 1935 delivery of Royal Blue Leyland TS7 Tigers were requisitioned by the War Department; just which one of them became the United States Army's military transport No 1826424 has gone unrecorded. It is quite likely that this vehicle was used to carry US personnel to the huge bombsite coach park at Crosshouse Quay, Southampton, in preparation for D-Day (6 June 1944).
Colin Morris collection

Left: Having heard that Bedford and Duple had co-operated to produce an elegant new coach, the OB model, Southern/Western National in July 1939 placed an order for the 26-seat version. Sadly World War 2 started that September, and when eight for WNOC and 11 for SNOC were duly delivered in 1940 they were instead found work not entirely suited to their luxurious interiors. Smartened up postwar, they were frequently employed on Royal Blue relief work; here SNOC's No 495 (DOD 544) waits within range of Victoria Coach Station for its turn to collect passengers for the West Country. *Roy Marshall / East Pennine Transport Group*

When Royal Blue express services recommenced after World War 2 Southern/Western National had to make do with the existing prewar vehicles, and it was not until 1948 that newly built replacements began to arrive. The newcomers were Bristol L chassis bodied by Beadle to a style developed from an original streamlined design created by Duple. Photographed working the Bournemouth–Bristol Associated Motorways service, No 1212 (JUO 944) was one of the first batch of 13 L6Bs delivered to WNOC. *Alan Lambert collection*

In 1922, at about the time time that Harry Rollings joined Elliott Bros in Holdenhurst Road, Bournemouth, so too did a young man called Eric Horobin. He was taken on as a driver of those sky-blue and solid-tyred charabancs featured so frequently in 'happy-holidaymaker' photographs taken before departures from The Square and collected upon return. Whereas Rollings had become Tours Manager for Hants & Dorset in 1935, Horobin had jumped ship somewhat earlier and in May 1932 had become Traffic Manager at Exeter for both Southern and Western National. Came World War 2, and by December 1944 the Allies had become so confident of victory in Europe that a Control Commission for Germany (Transport Division) had been formed — and Horobin was 'borrowed' from SNOC/WNOC to help set up Britain's contribution to that effort. After Germany's surrender in May

1945 he was sent there to supervise many aspects of the reinstatement of public land transport in all its varied forms in that country.

As a result of the vacancy created at Exeter, Eric Horobin was paid the honour of being replaced by two company officers — Roland Buszard as Traffic Manager (Operating) and Clement Preece as Traffic Manager (Commercial). When he heard of Preece's new appointment and title, one traffic commissioner congratulated him but enquired caustically 'Who ever heard of an un-commercial traffic manager?'

After Word War 2 had finally ground to a halt with the Allied victory over Japan in August 1945 there was an immediate indication from both the Ministry of War Transport and the Regional Transport Commissioners (both at this stage retaining their wartime titles) that those operators which had been obliged to stop running their express services in 1942 might now begin the process of reinstating them. For several reasons that did not mean that such activities could be resumed the following week. As prewar traffic-court procedures had shown, submitting applications, listening to all the submissions both for and against, and then, if successful, linking up the positive results from one traffic area to the next was a very long procedure. Much had changed from area to area. There could be no 'quick fix'.

An early imposed requirement for the resumption of such services was that the railway companies should be informed of any proposals and be given the opportunity to oppose them. At various points throughout the country, bus companies had frequently helped out when enemy activity had severed a railway line, so no great animosity was abroad. In Royal Blue's case such a proviso was not to cause too onerous a situation, because its proprietors were each 50% owned by railway companies — the Southern in the case of Southern National and the Great Western in the case of sister Western National. Both were proportionately represented upon the respective board of directors and were in every case party to the decision-making process about all the road-service activities planned or already activated. The main problem for Royal Blue was vehicles: whereas SNOC's and WNOC's stage-carriage fleets had continued to receive small batches of replacement rolling stock throughout the austere years of the war, understandably not one new Royal Blue coach chassis had been delivered in that period, for the very good reason that there was

latterly no work left for it to do. The Royal Blue coaches available for any restart were by that time in pretty poor shape, both inside and out. The main garage and workshops at Plymouth had been severely damaged by two very serious raids, and the Western National workshops had been forced to relocate to Southern National's equivalent premises at Bideford. Grossly overworked already, this 'central works' was in no position to address Royal Blue's needs as a priority. Much of the necessary refurbishment was therefore contracted out.

Nevertheless, when a tentative restart of express services proper — as compared with the two hands-full of vehicles which ran the six wartime emergency services centred upon Bournemouth — was finally launched in April 1946, some spruced-up prewar old-stagers reappeared in gradually increasing numbers in Bournemouth, Southampton, Portsmouth, Plymouth, Bristol and London, in each location running to their destination through scenes of war-torn devastation. Where rows of shops had once had cellars, the roads were in several places left like a raised causeway some 10ft above what had become the new ground level. As one Royal Blue driver remarked, 'It was like receiving a welcoming smile from a very elderly man with no teeth!' All very sad. Ilfracombe, in much better shape, also gained the beginnings of a restarted express service at the same time, while Penzance had its Royal Blue presence restored in June.

Optimistically, the new-vehicle order planned for deliveries in 1947 to SNOC/WNOC included a call for thirteen 32-seater Bristol luxury coaches for Royal Blue service at a total cost of £35,000. Not surprisingly, they were not delivered in that year, for manufacturers generally had yet to wind down their wartime activity and re-tool accordingly.

The refurbished and re-launched prewar coaches thus bore the entire responsibility for running the restored routes for the next two years — and an eye- and ear-catching sight and sound they made, too. Living on a route (Portsmouth–Southampton–Bournemouth) which never did stop running in World War 2, I found it fascinating to note, as the fleet began to build up once more, how many subtle differences there were in what was visually a fleet with 'standard' bodywork. A shorter wheelbase produced a short window amidships; some vehicles had tapered rear wings, others had not; some had doors at the rear, others at the front; there were Bristol radiators, AEC Regals and both 'button-nosed' and longer Covrad replacement radiators on Leyland Tigers; registration letters varied considerably, giving clues as to where their careers had begun. Even their voices differed also. Winding their way out of East Street in Titchfield and heading west up Southampton Hill, the diesel-powered coaches emitted a guttural rattle, whilst those with autovacs stained red by commercial rationed petrol, particularly the elderly Tigers, hissed audibly as they passed by, with a much sweeter note, but backfired without fail as they disappeared around the first right-hand bend. But they all seemed to say 'Here we are! We're Royal Blues and rather special — and what's more we're still on the road.' It really is surprising that I did not become a bus enthusiast.

It is not entirely true that Royal Blue received nothing new during World War 2. Just occcasionally there appeared on that self-same hill one or other of two coaches which proved to be a foretaste of what would eventually follow. These were two AEC Regals which had been rebodied by Duple in 1941 — see *Glory Days: Royal Blue* (2000). Their coachwork was streamlined and looked very special. The pattern for them had already been passed to Beadle at Dartford, where that firm's chief designer was already at work making subtle improvements upon its lines. The chosen chassis, however, was to be an uprated Bristol L with gracefully shaped and lowered radiator, and it was to be fitted with the new six-cylinder Bristol AVW engine.

In May 1948 the first examples to be delivered were at last gratefully received at the Rutland Road works in Bournemouth. The best place to hear their so-impressive start-up was 'down the chute' inside the coach station in The Square — a crackling roar followed by a reassuring feline 'tick-over' — and then some gentle revving, the first clue that many of the drivers liked the noise as well and enjoyed 'playing their engines', just as much as Clem Preece took pleasure in playing the church organ each Sunday at Clyst St Mary, near Exeter. Preece records, incidentally, that he was so thrilled that he was at last to receive some new Royal Blue vehicles that, when the first batch of L6Bs to be allocated to Exeter were expected, he walked five miles out of the city toward Honiton to meet them. Hopefully the first driver recognised him and took him on board. Preece must have had a soft spot for the location of that 'first sight', for he soon afterward bought a house thereabouts, joining the local horticultural society in the process. It took some while for his neighbours to discover how it was that his garden was completely transformed every few months!

During 1948 a total of 35 Bristol Ls (25 with Bristol engines and 10 with AEC units), all bodied by Beadle, joined the Royal Blue fleet. A further 10 L6Bs and three L6As — again bodied by Beadle — were delivered in 1949. The following year saw a further 10 L6Bs join the fleet, this time built by Duple — ironically to the standard set by Beadle.

That year of 1950 saw three pieces of legislation which would in the longer term affect the future of coach travel in all its forms. The most influential in the long run was the Finance Act 1950, which in effect let slip the monetary leash — and the aftermath was perhaps best illustrated by the contemporary cartoon figure of 'Mr Rising Price'.

SALISBURY EXETER
BASINGSTOKE SALISBURY
GUILDFORD SOUTHAMPTON
BASINGSTOKE WINCHESTER
BASINGSTOKE BLANDFORD
GUILDFORD WINCHESTER
AMESBURY TAUNTON
EXETER DORCHESTER
RELIEF CAR
ON HIRE TO
SOUTHERN NATIONAL
ON HIRE TO
WESTERN NATIONAL

BRISTOL CHELTENHAM
NEWBURY CHIPPENHAM
NEWBURY OXFORD
YEOVIL TAUNTON
BASINGSTOKE ANDOVER
BRIDPORT DORCHESTER
BLANDFORD SHERBORNE
TROWBRIDGE SALISBURY

CHIPPENHAM SALISBURY
SWINDON SALISBURY
SALISBURY SOUTHAMPTON
LYNDHURST SOUTHAMPTON
EASTLEIGH BASINGSTOKE
OXFORD STRATFORD-ON-AVON
WEYMOUTH SEATON
OXFORD LICHFIELD
SHAFTESBURY BATH
ALDERSHOT OXFORD
CALLINGTON ... RAMPTON

Lower-panel 'via' destination blind for Royal Blue Bristol L coaches.

Left: Twelve Bristol L6B chassis fitted with 31-seat Beadle coachwork for Royal Blue services were the first new coaches delivered postwar to Southern National, in 1948. With not too many miles on the clock, No 1221 (JUO 986) has arrived at Southdown's Hilsea garage on 20 February 1949, on service from Bournemouth to Hyde Park Road, Portsmouth. In the summer months particularly, SNOC/WNOC based some coaches and crew at Hilsea which — cheekily — they considered 'an outstation of Bournemouth'! *The Omnibus Society*

Below left: The Bournemouth–Southampton–Liverpool service had been started by Tourist Motor Coaches (Southampton) Ltd in 1930, primarily for the benefit of personnel in the shipping industries. Having been acquired by Tilling and placed in the care of SNOC/WNOC in 1934, the new 'Royal Blue' operated the service as part of the Associated Motorways network. Here SNOC's No 1235 (HOD 98), a Bristol L6A/Beadle of 1948, has arrived from Southampton via Oxford and Lichfield — and appears to have had its radiator recently topped up. *Ian Allan Library*

Below: When equal numbers of AEC Regals were delivered to Western and Southern National in 1937 for use as Royal Blue coaches, those for WNOC had been bodied by Mumford, those for SNOC by Duple. Just one of the latter was fitted with a new replacement body (by Duple), in 1941. All the others were updated in 1949 with new Beadle 31-seat coachwork, bringing them into visual conformity with the 32 new Bristol L6B and L6A coaches, also bodied by Beadle, delivered the previous year. Regal No 1054 (ETA 980) was captured arriving at Victoria from Westward Ho! *Andrew Waller collection*

Left: The start of the 1950s was boom-time for travel by express-service coaches nationwide. It was a time when the hiring-in of other operators' vehicles, at weekends in particular, to operate as additional 'relief cars', became an absolute necessity. The good relationship with Wilts & Dorset Motor Services Ltd, built up originally in the 1930s by Elliott Bros, meant that SNOC/WNOC had a ready and willing supply of good-quality vehicles from that source. Bristol L6B/Portsmouth Aviation 32-seater No 286 (FAM 3) was one of them. *Portsmouth Aviation / David Pennels collection*

Left: A summer scene at Hants & Dorset's Grosvenor Square garage in Southampton in 1950 — some five years before a proper departure and arrival station was opened on the other side of the building. The Southdown Leyland Tiger PS1/Beadle coach of 1948 *en route* to Brighton would have been officially 'on hire' to Royal Blue Services as far as Hilsea, whilst SNOC's AEC Regal/Beadle 31-seater No 1064 (ETA 958) would terminate at Hyde Park Road, Portsmouth. Both were operating ex Bournemouth, so presumably the latter was the 'relief car' on this trip. *Alan Lambert collection*

SALISBURY
TORQUAY
PAIGNTON
BOURNEMOUTH
EXETER
PLYMOUTH
LONDON KINGS CROSS
LONDON VICTORIA
PENZANCE
ILFRACOMBE
WEYMOUTH
WEYMOUTH & SWANAGE
NEWQUAY
St IVES
FALMOUTH
MINEHEAD
BUDE
LYNTON
SOUTHAMPTON
SWANAGE
PRIVATE
BIRMINGHAM
CHELTENHAM
WESTON-SUPER-MARE
BRISTOL
PORTSMOUTH
SOUTHAMPTON
OXFORD
BRIGHTON
COVENTRY
BATH
YEOVIL
LIVERPOOL
CHELTENHAM
FOR CONNECTING SERVICES
EXMOUTH
WINCHESTER
TAUNTON
St AUSTELL
PADSTOW
BARNSTAPLE
MANCHESTER
MEVAGISSEY
PARK PREWETT
SHAFTESBURY
HONITON
TROWBRIDGE
BOURNEMOUTH

Right: Associated Motorways routes originating in the Royal Blue territorial area were equally in need of reinforcement at weekends. Demand for extra seats became so heavy that the local Tilling (BTC) or BET subsidiary companies could not always satisfy the need, and on such occasions independent operators with good-quality vehicles were asked to help out. This Leyland Tiger PS1 of Basil Williams' Hants & Sussex — No 203 (GOT 185) of 1948 — with its well-appointed Duple A-type coachwork, proved up to the mark. *Colin Morris collection*

To a certain extent this had a restraining effect upon the number of people who could actually afford to buy their own cars — as they may well have been, in order to take advantage of the year's de-rationing of petrol (no-one had a diesel-engined car in those days) — and probably to some extent passengers carried on Royal Blue express services continued to rise. Thirdly, the long-standing restriction upon length (27ft 6in) imposed for single-deck public-service vehicles (PSVs) was relaxed to 30ft — just enough to provide four extra seats.

Right: One of the first Royal Blue examples of the Bristol LL6B — the longer version of the L, and the model that replaced it, No 1252 (LTA 731) had room for 37 passengers (six extra seats) in its Duple-built body. Here it has been shadowed to London from Exeter by WNOC's very first 'Queen Mary' ECW-bodied Bristol LWL6B, No 1310 (LTA 859). The latter was not only longer but, measuring 8ft across the beam, also 6in wider than the earlier L model. Both vehicles were new in 1951. *Alan Lambert*

Royal Blue immediately benefited, for SNOC/WNOC placed orders there and then for 24 Bristol LL6B coaches with 37-seat Duple bodywork built to the new length. These arrived in 1951, and by some enthusiasts with an eye for æsthetic niceties they were considered strong candidates for the title of 'most elegant coaches ever built'. Their arrival brought the number of vehicles in the Royal Blue fleet up to 130, and most contributed to the increased traffic of that year as many more thousands of people went 'up to town' to visit the 'Festival of Britain' from virtually every extremity of the Royal Blue network. Many of these new customers readily accepted that this would entail travelling long distances throughout the night in order to enjoy a full day at the exhibition. Thus a further source of regular custom had been discovered, and, although the numbers fell short of those who had visited the Festival, 'travel by night' became an established feature of Royal Blue activity.

Above: Bound for Salisbury via Basingstoke and Andover, Western National Bristol LL6B/Duple 37-seater No 1256 (LTA 735) of 1951 was at the time of this photograph a London Victoria-based vehicle in the hands of one of the numerous drivers also based in the capital. Quaintly, vehicles and crews domiciled there were deemed to constitute a subsidiary of the Bournemouth depot! The four-aperture destination display is rather unusual as set. *Andrew Waller collection*

Above right: Bristol LL6B No 1303 (LTA 741) was a 37-seat green-and-cream Duple-bodied coach — one of the last 10 half-cab coaches delivered to Western National. Their luxurious interiors made them ideal vehicles to fulfil their weekend role as 'relief cars' on Royal Blue and Associated Motorways express services. Both this car and the following Southdown Tiger are being shunted around to Samuelson's garage for a clean — and servicing if necessary. *Andrew Waller collection*

Above: Parked among fellow Royal Blue Bristols at Exeter is Western National's Bristol LL6B/Duple 37-seater coach No 1277 (LTA 865) of 1951. This nearside shot shows how the extra length of the LL model improved upon the gracious streamlined side elevation of the earlier model, producing arguably the most elegant Royal Blue coaches to grace the roads of England and Wales. The effect was reduced somewhat when the cream-top livery, better suited to full-fronted coaches, was introduced. *Alan Lambert collection*

One particularly sad event had occurred on 16 November 1950. Lee Fletcher, Traffic Superintendent for Royal Blue at the coach station in Bournemouth, had died after a very short illness. Fletcher had come from Lancashire with S. C. Bullock and Thomas Briggs in 1927 and had been employed by the reconstituted Tourist Coaches (Southampton) Ltd. When that firm had been acquired by Tilling in 1935 and split three ways he transferred to Southern/Western National and was in effect put in charge of Royal Blue's operational centre. To him had been answerable all those who worked for Royal Blue on the traffic side at Bournemouth and its summer satellite at Portsmouth. He was replaced in that post by George Foot.

Clem Preece had followed up his photographic-record efforts in war-torn Southampton by chancing his arm as a company 'photoshoot' artist in an effort to spruce up the publicity material published for Royal Blue Services. It had started, despite some scepticism about its potential value from those at the Exeter headquarters, when he took AEC Regal No 3631 (LJ 1519) and posed it in various attractive locations — not too difficult to find in picturesque Devon, but being in the right place to have the sun illuminating both the coach and the chosen glorious backdrop was never as easy as it sounds. Nevertheless, he secured several highly successful photographs of high definition at that time, even if aided by a little artistic titivation along the way. How he recruited the regular coach passengers sounds like something taken from the television series *The Apprentice*. A holiday camp in Torquay was asked to provide sufficient volunteer 'inmates' who were guaranteed a free coach tour to 'some beautiful locations' — provided that they turned out dressed in travelling clothes rather than their more usual beachwear.

The photographs were just black-and-white at that time but to Preece looked very impressive. He managed to slide them in front of Tilling Group Chairman Sir Frederick Heaton after the latter had been suitably wined and dined at a company dinner. He explained their planned purpose. To his relief Sir Frederick took the wind from the sails of those who believed such things to be an expensive waste of time, declaring within their earshot: 'That is what I call good publicity!' Thereafter everyone else thought so too.

The Associated Motorways network based at Cheltenham, together with Royal Blue's contribution toward it, had resumed operations post World War 2 soon after the restoration programme for Royal Blue itself started in 1946. This association from the beginning owed much to the initiative of H. R. Lapper, who had become Director and General Manager of Black & White Motorways Ltd in 1927, when he effectively took over from the founder of that company, George Readings. Whereas the latter had established the link between Cheltenham and London, under Lapper Black & White's coaches had set off in various directions (see *Glory Days: Black & White* by Kevin Lane, published 2003), thus establishing the concept of Cheltenham as a hub where passengers could find numerous timed connections. In 1930 control of the firm had been assumed by the Birmingham & Midland Motor Omnibus Co Ltd ('Midland Red'), at that time with the characterful Irishman O. C. Power at the helm. (The initials O. C. P. on correspondence in those days made anyone sit up and take notice.) Bristol Tramways (now in control of Greyhound) and The City of Oxford Motor Services Ltd had been brought into the fold soon afterward. R. H. Nicholls, the GWR's Superintendent of the Line, became Black & White's first Chairman. As personalities counted for a great deal at that time, Western National had 'an ear to the keyhole', in that Nicholls was, with effect from 21 February 1929, one of its founding directors. And when, in 1932, Western National assumed control of Bristol Tramways (see *Western National Omnibus Company*, 2008) its association with Black & White became rather more like 'a foot in the door'. Upon Nicholls' retirement from his chairmanship of Black & White, O. C. Power had replaced him; whilst H. R. Lapper continued as General Manager. When Associated Motorways came into being, in July 1934, Lapper became Chairman of its management committee — a position he was to hold until retirement in 1953. Western National and Southern National had become official members of the association upon their acquisition of Royal Blue Automobile Services in January 1935. Thus Clement Preece had represented 'Royal Blue' under two separate regimes since the date when he first undertook various negotiations upon the association's behalf. He became a member of its management committee and described its main function as a vehicular 'pulse

ROYAL BLUE
SERVICES

TIME TABLE 3ᴰ
Commencing 7th April, 1952 until 19th October, 1952 (inclusive).
Cancelling issue dated 22nd October, 1951.

operation'. To set these 'pulses' in motion —
in those days at 1-2pm and 4-4.30pm, at which
times there was a mass exodus of coaches to all
points of the compass — an inspector blew a
whistle, and off from Cheltenham Coach Station
they all sped.

Clem Preece was among those members of the
committee who undertook numerous test runs
aboard various coaches to check time intervals and
appropriate places for them to stop whilst on service
— always, of course with an eye to the best interests
of Royal Blue. It certainly paid good dividends for
Western and Southern National to have him
undertake such a role. Not in the least
shamefacedly, Preece admits that on one occasion
the management committee managed to complete
all its business in time to attend Cheltenham Races.
There he saw upon the card a horse called
Royal Blue, and its jockey was named Elliott
— clearly a cert. It came in last!

During the era of the much-liked
latter-day Royal Blue half-cab
coaches, SNOC and WNOC, as part
of the Tilling group of companies,
were in effect 'nationalised' (the
public-ownership version), becoming
the property of the state. Principally
because it became necessary for
Government to employ the senior
officers of Tilling to organise and
indeed run the nationalised arm
of the bus industry as 'The Tilling
Association', the devotees of travel
by Royal Blue noticed no changes
whatsoever, either to the vehicles or
to their established travel routines.
'Leave well that runs well' appeared
to be the Government's position.
The Royal Blue Bristol Ls and LLs
did just that and, in the main,
survived in the employ of
Southern/Western National
until withdrawal in 1961
and 1964 respectively.

Left: Hants & Dorset's
coach station in Bedford Place,
Southampton, was designed
by the company's architect,
H. J. Starkey, in 1935.
Southern/Western National's
Royal Blue express services and
those of Associated Motorways
were granted booking facilities
therein in return for a percentage
of the receipts. The departure
bays for express services
(to the right of the building)
were constructed by H. G. Ross
& Sons Ltd two decades later,
coming into operation
on 25 August 1955.
Colin Morris collection

Left: An unusual contribution to
the 1958 summer-Saturday relief
effort was this Crossley SD42
of Marchwood Motorways Ltd.
It has turned up at Hants &
Dorset's Bedford Place
'Coach Station' to act as a
Royal Blue back-up vehicle
on the Bournemouth–Yeovil–
Weston-super-Mare service.
Someone has gone into the
office to fetch an 'on hire'
sticker to go in the front
window. At this early stage in its
history Marchwood Motorways
ran a fleet of second-hand
vehicles in the motley colours
of their original owners.
*Harold Stevens / Colin Morris
collection*

Above: The end of the line at Bideford depot in June 1963 for the 1250 (LTA 7xx) batch of Bristol LL6B coaches new in 1951. These were the stretched versions of the earlier Bristol L-type coaches for Royal Blue and as 37-seaters provided four more seats within their elongated and elegant Duple bodywork. When new all these vehicles featured the pre-WW2 livery pattern whereby the roofs also were painted royal blue. That arrangement had come to an end in 1953 when this 'cream-top' scheme was adopted, in an attempt — as elsewhere within the Tilling Group — to brighten things up. *C. L. Caddy collection*

Right: Bristol LL6B/Duple coach No 1269 (LTA 898) of Southern National proved somewhat longer-lived after withdrawal than most of its contemporaries. As the property of R. L. Pryor of Bournemouth, in the summer of 1967 it turned up in Paris, where it posed in the company of those pig-nosed Renault buses with nodding indicators. Pryor, himself an archæologist, passed it on to the Bournemouth Archæology Society, in whose care — despite the mud — it was photographed in Castle Lane in 26 January 1969. Suitably cleaned, it visited the Yeovil gathering in 1982. *C. L. Caddy*

Left and below left: Among the batch of coaches put up for sale at Bideford in 1963 had been No 1250 (LTA 729), the first Bristol LL6B/Duple Royal Blue coach. Despite being allocated to Western National it was a regular performer on service P between Bournemouth and Ilfracombe (see illustration in *Glory Days: Royal Blue*). After withdrawal it spent three years in the vicinity of Exmoor with Sherrin's of Carhampton before ultimately finding its way into the West Country Historic Omnibus & Transport Trust collection; it was then lovingly restored by owner Colin Billington, pictured here at the wheel as the vehicle sweeps into West Point, Exeter, at the conclusion of a commemorative run from Cheltenham in September 2006.
Colin Morris (both)

Below: In the mid-1950s both Southern and Western National initiated a process of ensuring that those of its coaches likely to be employed at weekends as relief vehicles for Royal Blue express services would be painted in royal blue and cream. This followed several incidences of irritable customers complaining that they had paid to travel by 'Royal Blue' only to have a green-and-cream coach turn up. In fact the latter were just as luxurious, being LL6Bs bodied (by Duple) to a similar pattern as 37-seaters. Compare SNOC's No 1324 (LTA 958) with LTA 729 of the same year.
Colin Morris

Although the full-fronted Bristol LWL/ECW 'Queen Mary' design went some way toward satisfying the desire for modernity prevalent in the early 1950s — and made the vehicle look more imposing — the length and seating capacity were no greater than those of the concurrent LL model. Thus Southern National No 1332 (LTA 927) and its fellows were very much interim models pending the arrival of the Bristol LS. Although the LWLs were much used as Royal Blue relief cars, none wore the familiar blue livery.
F. G. Reynolds

When the joint Hants & Dorset/Royal Blue bus/coach station in Bournemouth was being built, in 1930, the contractors took care to construct the retaining walls of the entrance and exit ramps in reinforced concrete rather than more-flimsy layers of brick, in case a vehicle collided with them. In those days the maximum permitted width of a PSV had been 7ft 6in, so there was not too high a chance that this would happen. Not recorded in any official minute, however, is that when the 1950 legislation permitted single-decked PSVs to be built to a length of 30ft, it also decreed that all PSVs could, if so desired, be 8ft wide. Southern and Western National immediately took advantage of both for both double- and single-deck vehicles in their green-and-cream fleets but eschewed the latter for Royal Blue. So, when the Bristol LL6Bs had arrived they had been built to the earlier and narrower width. It seems highly likely that the management was rather anxious about the clearance on the coach-station ramps.

It is true that there were always rather more red and green scrape-marks than blue, left upon the ramp walls by hired-in relief coaches belonging to other firms. Whatever, the anxiety was forcibly dispelled when the Bristol LL model was replaced upon the market by something completely new.

For many years Royal Blue coaches and those of other operators part of that group running under the auspices of Associated Motorways had shared duties with the much more modern-looking full-fronted vehicles of Midland Red. Now all the Tilling members of that association (and those Tilling firms which were not) were about to be brought up to date. Despite earlier having walked several miles to meet those early Bristol L types, Clement Preece now described vehicles of their configuration as 'the half-cab type, in which the driver sat in a kind of chicken coop beside the engine'.

Based on a prototype built in 1950, the Bristol LS (Light Saloon) coach entered service with Royal Blue in 1952. It was built as an underfloor-engined vehicle of integral construction in concert with Eastern Coach Works Ltd, both firms being now part of the British Transport Commission's portfolio. The chassis frame, of all-welded steel construction, incorporated the underframe for the bodywork, which in turn needed the body superstructure (built the width of the country away, in Lowestoft) to complete what was a vehicle of box-girder construction, combining strength and lightness. This new coach was full-fronted, and, as the steered wheels were set well back, the driver now 'sat with the passengers', the entrance/exit door being located ahead of the front axle. The only snag about the latter arrangement was that the door required handling with care because it swung outwards (see illustration). A feature of the first examples for Royal Blue was that the 'five each side' glazed windows along the cove panels on the standard model were replaced by five metal panels incorporating the four permanent plates which spelled '**ROYAL BLUE COACH SERVICE**'. In addition the first LS coaches continued to feature the traditional streamlined roof-mounted luggage-rack with retractable steps at the rear to reach it. At the front the early examples also featured curved corner glazing designed to improve forward vision for the passengers, but in practice this played tricks with the light, distracting drivers somewhat.

Left: Pictured at Southern National's Radipole garage in Weymouth on 6 October 1965 are a pair of that company's Bristol LWL6B/ECW 37-seat coaches of 1951, Nos 1335/6 (LTA 930/1). Those delivered to both WNOC and SNOC were their first coaches built to the newly permitted width of 8ft. (For some other companies, early examples were delivered on remaining stocks of 7ft 6in wide chassis.) 'Queen Marys' or 'Brabazons', as they were nicknamed, were frequently called upon to provide relief journeys for weekend Royal Blue services, these two examples included. *C. L. Caddy*

Left: Bedford OB/Duple No 1404 (HOD 83) was new in 1949 as a 29-seat green-and-cream coach for WNOC. From 1953 onward the company began altering the vehicles of this large batch to 27-seaters and repainting them in Royal Blue livery. No 1404 was among the last to be so treated, in 1957. It is pictured outside the Trevol Road, Torpoint, garage occupied originally by the Cornwall Motor Transport arm of the Devon Motor Transport Co Ltd, which premises passed to NOTC and thence to Western National upon its formation in 1929. *C. L. Caddy collection*

Right: In July 1952 both Western and Southern National received their first examples of the new integrally constructed Bristol/ECW LS coach — each painted in Royal Blue colours and incorporating the traditional roof rack for luggage. By the end of that year WNOC (LTA registrations) and SNOC (MOD) had seven apiece. No 1291 (MOD 978) was photographed at Stewarts Park whilst in the care of the Eastern National Preservation Group. At some stage in its career it has acquired the standard Bristol-ECW badge at the front instead of its original 'winged bomb' device. *Duncan Bulmer*

Below: The regulator at Hants & Dorset Motor Services' newly enlarged Fareham bus station stands like a ringmaster at the centre of things, his eye upon two Southdown double-deckers awaiting the off for Portsmouth and Southsea. Behind him one of the 1952 batch of Royal Blue LS integrals pauses awhile *en route* to Margate (Kent) on a service now operated jointly with Southdown and East Kent. As early as January 1935 Clement Preece had been negotiating with Hants & Dorset over the price to be charged for his coaches' entering this station. *Colin Morris collection*

Nevertheless, when this early version of the LS was introduced both drivers and passengers liked the performance available from the six-cylinder Gardner engine, as well as the comfortable riding characteristics and the very luxurious seating, which all together made them ideal for the long journeys they were designed to undertake. They were also, from the Western and Southern National companies' point of view, reasonably economical to run, the manufacturers' prototype having achieved a fuel-consumption figure of 16.8 miles per gallon on test whilst still in chassis form before completion. The main monetary problem for the two operating companies was 'Mr Rising Price' — a complete new LS coach cost exactly £4,000 in 1952. By 1957 that price had risen to £4,950, and that had little to do with extra fitments to the model or general improvements to the vehicle. On the contrary, the modifications to the type should have made it less expensive to produce for Royal Blue. First, the elegant but in practical terms unsatisfactory quarterlights were dispensed with on following examples. Secondly, in an attempt to cut out the frills, someone at Exeter must have suggested that the traditional roof rack and chromium steps to reach it could go, to be replaced by the standard, glazed cove panels, as produced for every other customer for the model. One can imagine Clem Preece being rather saddened. All to little avail, however, for the price continued to rise. The LS enjoyed a relatively

long life in the Royal Blue fleet, even those with the now old-fashioned roof rack (which tended no longer to be used anyway) lasting until 1969. That longevity was most likely caused in part by that out-swinging door, which made them unsuitable for downgrading for later use as stage-carriage buses.

Right: At a time when Royal Blue's newly delivered LS coaches were still displaying 'ROYAL BLUE COACH SERVICES' in permanent form along the above-window cove panels, Southern and Western National's contemporary green-and-cream LS coaches instead featured large curved 'vista' windows, five on each side. Thus fitted, these vehicles made ideal Royal Blue route-extension equipment. Recorded in its last year in that role, SNOC's No 1376 (OTT 85) of 1953 prepares to take passengers onward from Bridport to Seaton on 19 July 1969. *Alan Lambert*

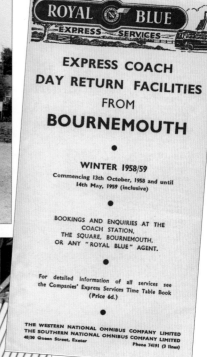

Left: This Royal Blue coach, Bristol LS/ECW 41-seater No 1299 (OTT 98), delivered to Southern National in September 1953, was the last built with the traditional streamlined roof-rack and 'identification and purpose' lettering along the cove panels at each side. It was also the last Royal Blue to feature the 'winged bomb' embellishment at the front, a modified version bearing a Bristol-ECW badge replacing it thereafter. *M. P. Rowledge*

The next model purchased for service with Royal Blue was the Bristol MW (Medium Weight) type, produced, once again, in conjunction with Eastern Coach Works, but their integral venture was discontinued, largely because each underframe produced at Bristol had to be specially reinforced to undertake the long journey to Lowestoft — a rather wasteful expense in a parlous financial climate. Instead the MW was built in the traditional manner, with separate chassis and bodywork. However, advanced technology and quality of material employed meant that the MW actually weighed less than the preceding LS. One might expect, therefore, that the performance of the MW would have been the more spritely. Not so; driver Howard Evans recalls: 'The old LS was, apart from dynamo problems, no trouble at all, and that was particularly so with my more usual one at Bude, No 1365 (OTT 74), and, since they were heavier than the MW, they actually rode better once they really got going, but from standstill the LS was very, very flat by comparison. On the other hand the MWs were tremendously slow on dual-carriageways and motorways — 52 miles per hour was their maximum speed. I think it was Western National policy to govern them down so they wouldn't go any faster.

Coming home from London on Sunday night you'd be down to second gear coming up Yarcombe Hill [just north of Chard] and on Telegraph Hill [south of Exeter] — if the gearstick stayed in you were laughing. I was actually coming in from Okehampton to Exeter one Saturday night and at Pocombe Bridge, over the Alphin Brook, I had to do a snatched change from first to second — always a difficult thing to do — and the gear-stick broke off. We were stuck there with about ten miles of traffic behind us.'

Having said that, Evans concluded his assessment of the MW as follows: 'For the driver they were totally abysmal but were comfortable and utterly reliable — I did a whole summer season with them from Bude — 168 days on the trot without a day off, same coaches, Nos 2240/1, £36 per week, 104 pay hours. Bargain! And those two MWs were utterly reliable.'

The year of the introduction of the Bristol MW (which type ushered into the Royal Blue fleet a new 'cream top' livery — all-cream above the waistrail — which was applied retrospectively to other vehicles remaining in the fleet) was also the year when the newly enlarged Bournemouth bus and coach station was opened.

Above left: Awaiting the mass exodus from Black & White Motorways' Cheltenham Coach Station on 18 May 1964 is one of the first Royal Blue Bristol LS6G/ECW coaches built without a roof-rack. Now in 1957, it was one of a batch of 12, shared equally between WNOC and SNOC, which featured the cove lights previously fitted only to those coaches officially 'hired in'. No 2208 (VDV 751) was due to depart for Plymouth as part of Royal Blue's contribution to Associated Motorways. *Edward G. Hodgkins*

Weymouth, the destination for a Southern National express service in London in the days before SNOC/WNOC acquired title to the Royal Blue brand, was the home-base for this Bristol MW6G/ECW, pictured having off-loaded its passengers at London's Victoria Coach Station. SNOC's No 2220 (XUO 730) was one of the 27-strong 1958 SNOC/WNOC intake of MW coaches, of which 14 belonged to the latter.
Alan Lambert collection

The express coaches now entered the station down the left-hand chute and proceeded toward their new stands in a much bigger area constructed beneath an equally enlarged standing area at ground level for Hants & Dorset's stage-carriage buses and a departure-point for its excursions and tours coaches. The Royal Blue coaches and their many duplicates then departed from the depths by heading straight on and exiting into Exeter Lane to the south of the station, before making two right turns to regain access to The Square.

The Bristol MW, which remained in production until 1967 (as coaches for Southern and Western National, but painted in Royal Blue colours for easy recognition when used as express-route duplicates), had been bodied by ECW in three distinct styles: the first visually resembled the earlier LS, but with a large air intake in the front dash; the second was without an indicator above the windscreen (but two beneath) plus a stepped waistline toward the rear of each side; whilst the third was a much-remodelled and modernised design.

Howard Evans, meanwhile, had been taken on as a driver at Bude by Inspector Jack Galliford. His elevation from stage-carriage driver to the man behind the wheel of a Royal Blue coach was quite rapid, and he soon found himself being asked to bring a London Victoria-bound vehicle up from Polzeath to Bude via Port Isaac, Delabole, Tintagel and Boscastle; the coach was then taken on to Exeter and thence direct to Victoria by an experienced driver based at Bude. 'This service was the Saturday-only service from Polzeath to London. The Bude driver worked back on Sunday as a duplicate to the many services that left London for several destinations in Cornwall. There was a corresponding duty where a Bude driver who'd operated up to London as a duplicate on Friday worked the 07.30 from Victoria to Polzeath as far as Bude, then an overtime duty took the vehicle as far as required.' If there were no more passengers the driver was lucky and had a short trip.

'When I started operating on that run up to the capital it involved a duplicate to Victoria on Thursdays and a whole day kicking heels until midnight — and arriving in Exeter at 7.30 in the morning. Very often there would be so many coaches in Paris Street that they were loading on the approach roads. I had four departures to Bude on busy Saturdays, with many private operators running duplicates called in to go to various parts of Devon and Cornwall. On arrival in Bude at 9.30am

Left: Bristol MW6G/ECW coaches for Royal Blue with more-spacious 39-seat arrangement first appeared in 1960 with a batch of 12 shared equally between SNOC/WNOC. This vehicle, No 2254 (59 GUO), was the first of an additional 16 — again divided equally — delivered for Royal Blue service the following year. It was photographed at Yeovil on 5 August 1964 whilst on route P (Bournemouth–Taunton–Ilfracombe). Yeovil Town station was a recognised passenger-exchange point. *Alan Lambert*

Below: They looked very much the same but structurally were very different; the Bristol LS was of integral construction, whereby the subframe relied to a great extent upon the body for its structural rigidity. The Bristol MW (Medium Weight) was of conventional body-on-chassis construction yet actually weighed less. LS6G No 1293 (OTT 92) and MW6G No 2261 (66 GUO) were photographed in Newquay bus station in September 1963. *John Callow*

the vehicle was fuelled, cleaned and made ready for me to take back to London on the night service departing at 8pm from Bude [and] getting to Victoria Coach Station at 6.30 on Sunday morning. London used to be dead at that time on a Sunday, and I used to go to a friend's house to stay until Monday, ready for another duplicate to Exeter. I did get caught for St Austell and Falmouth a couple of times, and that made a very long day by the time I got back to Bude.

'I was on duty that night in the July 1968 floods at Fenney Bridges [when the River Otter overflowed], and this involved a diversion back to Exeter and then up the A38 via Taunton, arriving three hours late in London. On the way back we were lucky to get through at all: there were dead chickens, a couple of sheep and fallen trees floating about. On that return trip we got flagged down by a London-bound Royal Blue coach, and the driver told us that the Police were sending the Cornwall-bound coaches via Taunton — and that involved a very long diversion, so we all put up "Exeter" on the blind, and when we got to Chard the police let us go via Axminster to Exeter. We arrived on time, and I think the Exeter inspectors still don't know how we did that.

Above: Most of the passengers have gone for tea and cakes at the cafeteria in Yeovil Town station as a typical weekend 'first reserve' vehicle waits nearby in October 1963. Western National No 1389 (258 KTA), a Bristol MW6G /ECW 39-seater delivered in 1962, was one of a batch of 13 which, along with a pair for Southern National, were the last coaches received in green and cream. They seem to have performed well, and in 1970 all were promoted to the Royal Blue fleet proper, being repainted accordingly. *C. L. Caddy*

Right: An ex-Silver Star Leyland Tiger Cub PSUC1/2, Western National No 3802 (KMW 644) about to perform one of its first duties for its new owner, on 20 July 1963. Moreover it is, as originally intended, fulfilling the role of a Royal Blue coach on an extension of route X (Exeter–Bournemouth–Hilsea–Reigate–Maidstone–Gillingham [Kent]), which east of Bournemouth was operated jointly with The Maidstone & District Motor Services Ltd. *R. B. Partridge*

'On one very busy night at Victoria an inspector noticed after a count that I only had 38 passengers on a 39-seater coach, and I said: "Yes, that's right." He said: "Well, I want that seat." I replied: "You can't have it — the lady in the front always buys two tickets because she's so big she needs to sit on her own." She was a regular passenger and used to travel every fortnight on the two front seats.

'I had a grim night once when the electrics on the coach failed and I had to follow the vehicle in front with rapidly failing side lights. The coach I successfully followed was driven by Alfie Mutter, who later became an inspector at Exeter. If he saw a new driver aboard a coach he used to stand beside the door and say to all those about to board: "You'll have to speak up — this driver's deaf," so every passenger that got on bawled at the alarmed novice: "TAUNTON, PLEASE!" He must have thought they'd all gone mad!

'I arrived at Victoria one Friday evening after a very good trip up and was unloading the boot when I saw a very well dressed gentleman with a ten-bob [50p] note in his hand — I anticipated a tip — waiting for his case. This was a soft leather morocco-bound affair. Unfortunately the fire-extinguisher had leaked, and the acid had eaten through the case and most of his clothes. No tip, and a lot of writing!'

When, in 1963, Wilts & Dorset Motor Services Ltd purchased the services and vehicles of Silver Star of Porton Down, Royal Blue's age-old association with the Salisbury-based company came once again into play. Whilst the majority of the Silver Star fleet was subsumed by that of W&D, seven were passed on forthwith to Western National, which painted them in royal blue and cream ready for either express or tours work, primarily from Exeter. Royal Blue drivers generally enjoyed the experience of getting behind the wheel of something new, and the Leyland Tiger Cubs and one Royal Tiger in this seven-strong additional fleet were sporty enough to live up to their expectations. Although not adorned with Royal Blue fleetnames, they always seemed to display that title in one destination aperture and frequently turned up on their own account, undertaking express duties as far afield as Penzance, London and Gillingham (Kent). However, as with most non-standard vehicles in any operator's fleet, their stay with Western National was rather short. Nevertheless, they had served as a foretaste of what was to come and provided a 'different' experience upon the road.

The converse applied to an interesting experience for Alan Lambert, at this time based at Southdown's Hyde Park Road depot in Portsmouth. He was asked to take a Royal Blue Bristol some five miles up the road to Hilsea depot, where such vehicles were parked for the night. The MW incorporated an 'interesting' overdrive fifth gear, unknown to Southdown, and here was an opportunity for him to experiment. Sailing along up Northern Parade he engaged the exciting fifth gear. Unfortunately no-one had told him that this magical gear could not be disengaged at less than about 40mph. To the consternation of the following traffic the MW rolled gently to a standstill, which then enabled second gear to be selected. Sorted!

Hyde Park Road depot was the scene of an eyebrow-raising encounter one summer Saturday in 1962 when a Leyland Tiger Cub of Basil Williams' Southern Motorways fleet turned up to act as yet another duplicate for an Associated Motorways trip to Cheltenham. Never in good odour with Southdown, particularly in his earlier Hants & Sussex days, Williams had his dismayed driver ordered by an incandescent Southdown official to remove the vehicle immediately to the street outside. That left the unfortunate local Royal Blue inspector, Bill Redfern, with the task of leading the bemused passengers outside to board the vehicle. Working on behalf of Associated Motorways (which was not amused by this incident) was clearly not always as straightforward as it may have seemed.

Throughout this period Royal Blue drivers and passengers continued to use the long-established comfort and refreshment stops across the network of routes, some of which went back to Elliott Bros days. The 'Cart & Horses' at King's Worthy had been dropped from the list as early as the 'Thirties following the opening of Winchester coach station, but surviving to the end of Royal Blue days were such time-

honoured pull-ins as those along the spinal Cornwall–London route: a big café at Tregadillett, two miles west of Launceston at the junction of the A30 and A395; Lewdown Services, where a coach from London to St Ives would take it over at 3 o'clock in the morning, meaning a free breakfast and a free packet of Woodbine cigarettes for the driver; on the early run up from Polzeath the 'Judge Jeffreys' at Crockernwell, on the northern fringe of Dartmoor Forest, where the driver got a free lunch and then bypassed Exeter, his next stop the 'Cribbage Hut' on the A30 near Fovant, Wilts (not too far from the Military Badges carved in the chalk hillside), which also served as a lunch stop for coaches going west; then it was on to the 'Toby Jug' near Guildford, described as 'a colossal coach stop'. In addition, going back westward were the 'Swan' at Hartley Wintney, Hants, where a driver received a free sandwich and a cup of coffee; the 'Druids' at Amesbury, Wilts (free afternoon tea), and, according to the time of day, a free meal of some sort at the 'Turk's Head', near Honiton, Devon. Accumulatively these rewards for having brought in a full load of hungry passengers represented a considerable daily saving in the dietary budget of Royal Blue's knights of the road.

When Douglas Mackenzie and Alfred Cannon founded Southdown in 1915 they planned to call it 'South Coast Motor Services Ltd', but at the last minute Companies House objected, because 'South Coast' had already been bagged, and 'Southdown' was substituted. Big smiles at Brighton, then, when, years later, the 'South Coast Express' to Bournemouth was established. Picking up passengers in Hove in 1956, Southdown Leyland Tiger Cub/Beadle No 1051 (RUF 51), new earlier that year, would be on hire to Royal Blue west of Portsmouth.
Alan Lambert collection

Right: No 1279 (LTA 867) created something of a stir when it was delivered in 1952. It was Western National's first full-fronted Royal Blue coach — a Bristol LS6G/ECW 41-seater, and, just as Elliott Bros' revolutionary AEC Q coaches of two decades previously, soon had passengers clamouring to come aboard. Even the drivers were keen to 'have a go'. This pioneer vehicle was photographed at Taunton on 4 June 1966, during its last summer season for Royal Blue. *C. L. Caddy*

Below: The device comprising a winged and dust-trailed wheel, with 'N' (for National) at the centre and 'SOUTHERN NATIONAL' or 'WESTERN NATIONAL' around the rim, was applied to Royal Blue coaches as soon as title to that brand was acquired from Elliott Bros (Bournemouth) Ltd in 1935. It survived in one form or another to be worn upon the sides of the Bristol LS coaches of the 1950s and the MWs of the following decade, but in the mid-1960s someone at Exeter clearly decided, that, from a design point of view, it was now *passé*. *Mike Stephens*

In 1963 arrived the last 10 MW6G coaches to join the Royal Blue fleet proper, all bar two the property of Southern National. They were followed in 1964 by a thoroughly new vehicle which had taken advantage of recent legislation permitting the increased dimensions of 36ft x 8ft 2½in. This was Bristol's RELH6G model, with long wheelbase, high chassis frame and rear-mounted six-cylinder Gardner engine — and, with ECW's specially designed coachwork, a real beauty. Fourteen joined the Royal Blue fleet that year, to be followed by a further six in 1967. All 20 had been fitted from new with the manual gearboxes with which Royal Blue drivers and fitters were thoroughly familiar. All those delivered afterward were equipped with semi-automatic 'boxes, a change designed to make life easier for the driver. Both types ran considerably more freely than the earlier models; as one ex-driver recalled, 'You were in seventh heaven if you were allocated an RE in MW days!'

At first, however, there was a slight snag. The earlier REs — the stick-change ones, as the drivers described them — were 'really good and went very well', and the Southern and Western National fitters, brought up on generations of manual gearboxes, really knew what to do if anything went the slightest bit wrong with them. It seems to have escaped someone's notice that these stalwart and essential members of the Royal Blue organisation would need some preparatory instruction in the maintenance of the new semi-automatic equipment, for when the REs thus equipped entered service they could not be sent out on service after daylight hours in case they broke down, there being at that time an insufficient number of night fitters competent to sort them out. 'So, for a while, if you were allotted an RE for a night-service run, it had to be a stick-change model.'

Photographed at Radipole garage in Weymouth following transfer to Southern National's care, Bristol LS6G/ ECW No 2201 (OTT 44) was originally a Western National vehicle. A 41-seater when delivered in 1953, it was downseated to 39 in 1961, after receiving its 'cream top'. The batch of which this coach was a part was the last to feature the traditional Royal Blue roof-mounted luggage-rack, reached by means of retractable steps at the rear. *C. L. Caddy*

For many years there was a major Royal Blue exchange-point in operation at Yeovil Town station. Within the building also were a well-run canteen and a Royal Blue office for the locally based inspector. During the MW and RE period particularly, that post was held by the affectionately nicknamed 'Welly-Boot Fred'. Whatever the weather, summer or winter, he wore wellington boots. 'And he was as good as gold, because you'd back your RE into the parking bay, and he'd come up and say: "I've got six passengers for you; how many off?" I'd tell him, and then he'd say: "You go and have a cup of tea, and I'll do the luggage," and he'd get the trolley out and do everything necessary to bring about a smooth exchange of passengers. At night, however, the station building was closed. When, for instance, we came into the forecourt at five in the morning we'd already stopped at Salisbury; but there was always someone who needed another comfort stop, and the schedule gave us time to do that. So we'd swing around and stop beside a field on the station approach and say something like: "If you wish to go into the field to have a cigarette or something, we're here for ten minutes; it's gentlemen to the left and ladies to the right — and mind the stinging-nettles!"

That was one of the things about those days — many of the passengers smoked, and, despite the company rules and legislation against it, several drivers had a crafty smoke as well. Indeed, when they first put those little red notices in the windows beside the four back rows of seats showing where you were allowed to smoke, old Driver Griffiths said: "How the 'ell can I drive the coach from back 'ere, then?"'

Clement Preece retired on 31 March 1965. Throughout the period up to that date he had continued to represent the interests of Royal Blue and Associated Motorways, both in and out of the traffic courts. His proudest achievement latterly, as recorded in his autobiography, was to 'complete' the Royal Blue network by adding a route 'designed to serve the north-western suburbs of London. The northern terminus was Hitchin, and the southern Salisbury. Here the main Royal Blue routes from London would be joined.' He established picking-up and setting-down points at Luton, Hemel Hempstead, Amersham and Slough, among others. He then cleared his desk, after a job done very well indeed, and concentrated on playing the church organ — and by all accounts he did that just as well.

In Hants & Dorset territory, a Royal Blue coach with traditional roof pannier has off-loaded its passengers from Barnstaple at Bournemouth Coach Station in The Square and is pictured running light for servicing at the Rutland Road works. In order to avoid a strenuous climb up Richmond Hill the fitter at the wheel has taken No 2202 (OTT 45), a Bristol LS6G new to Western National in 1953, along Bath Road and beside Bournemouth's large telephone exchange to turn left at The Lansdowne. *Mike Stephens*

Left: None too considerately parked in Newquay bus station, with a Southern National K5G double-decker blocked in beside it, is a Bristol LS6G/ECW 39 seater (originally 41 when new in 1957), seemingly at rest after running back light from Helston. A Western National vehicle (which might explain the parking), No 2203 (VDV 746) would be withdrawn in 1970, thereafter seeing further service — along with several other coaches of its batch — in the employ of Morris Bros, of Swansea. *Mike Stephens*

Left: Departing Salisbury coach station and falling in line with a fascinating cavalcade of 1960s vehicles (including Morris Minors, a Ford Anglia and a classic pea-green Mini van) leaving the adjacent car park, is a smart Royal Blue Bristol MW6G owned by Western National, No 2240 (XUO 723) of 1958. It was to serve as a Royal Blue express coach until 1973, when it gained a life-extension through conversion into a one-man-operated green-and-white bus for stage-carriage work. *Mike Stephens*

61

Right: Although Royal Blue enjoyed running rights beyond Hilsea as far as Brighton, as a matter of courtesy this vehicle bears a red-on-white 'South Coast Express' sticker in the windscreen, acknowledging that it was in Southdown territory.
En route to Bournemouth via Bognor Regis, Fareham and Southampton on 27 March 1966, WNOC's No 2272 (747 MDV), a 1963 Bristol MW6G/ECW 39-seater with stepped waistline, takes a short rest in Littlehampton, Sussex. *C. L. Caddy*

Below: One flew east, one flew west; two Bristol MW6G/ECW 39-seater coaches depart from the Swan Hotel, Hartley Wintney (Hants), refreshment stop at 10.30am on 26 June 1966 — a Sunday morning — to rejoin the A30, that famous road between London and Land's End. No 2244 (623 DDV) of 1960 is about to turn east for London Victoria, whilst its older sister, No 2237 (XUO 720) of 1958, prepares to head in the opposite direction, to Southampton and Bournemouth, having left Victoria at 8.30am. *Mike Stephens*

Left: No 3802 (KMW 644) was one of a pair of Leyland Tiger Cubs with 41-seat Harrington coachwork new in June 1954 to Silver Star Motor Services, of Porton Down, Wiltshire. When, in June 1963, that firm was acquired by Wilts & Dorset Motor Services Ltd, seven of its vehicles were passed forthwith to Western National, where they were repainted blue and cream for use primarily upon Royal Blue express-relief work. On this occasion, however, in the summer of 1966, No 3802 has been selected to undertake a tour from Plymouth. *C. L. Caddy*

Left: Ex-Silver Star (and Wilts & Dorset) Leyland Tiger Cub/Harrington 41-seater No 3804 (MMR 552), suitably painted for Royal Blue express duties, has instead found its way to Western National's Trevol Road premises at Torpoint in readiness for some private-hire work. The curious peaked dome on this vehicle and its ex-Wiltshire companions previously sported the 'silver star' trademark of their original owner. The picture was taken in June 1966, by which time this vehicle had just one more year to serve with WNOC. *C. L. Caddy*

Right: The later style of bodywork devised by ECW for the Bristol MW6G coach is here recorded by an historian and photographer held in high regard in the West Country. No 1413 (EDV 543D), new to Southern National in 1966, was one of a batch of eight, which, along with nine received by Western National, were delivered in Royal Blue livery for use as relief cars, although, as suggested by the destination indicator, they were equally likely to be employed on upmarket tours. *R. C. Sambourne*

Below: Elliott Bros having long ago established a working relationship with Wilts & Dorset Motor Services Ltd, SNOC/WNOC reaped the benefit for many years thereafter. At Salisbury coach station, in the company of a Bristol Greyhound Bristol RELH (*left*) are two 1962-vintage Wilts & Dorset MW6G coaches with the later style of ECW bodywork. 'On hire' to Royal Blue, Nos 716 (674 AAM) and 718 (130 AMW) are about to part company, heading to Paignton and Taunton respectively. *David Pennels collection*

Below: Loading passengers from Royal Blue services ex London and elsewhere for onward transit to destinations in the West Country, a pair of Grey Cars AEC Reliance coaches stand in a damp Paris Street coach station in Exeter. The driver of the Willowbrook-bodied 41-seater, Devon General No 965 (965 HTT), has yet to remove 'EXCURSION AND TOUR' from the destination display, although the 'ROYAL BLUE' sticker inside the windscreen reveals that his trip will see him piloting this attractive vehicle to St Ives. *Alan Lambert collection*

Left: Western National No 2204 (VDV 747), a Bristol LS6G/ECW, was the second vehicle in a batch of 12 which were the first Royal Blue coaches to dispense with roof-mounted luggage-racks and 'information' apertures above the side windows, sporting instead clear 'vista'-style roof-lights. Delivered in 1957 as a 41-seater, it was downseated to 39 in 1964 and is pictured departing Salisbury coach station on a short-working to Paignton on route X3 — a typical weekend duty — in July 1968. *Mike Stephens*

Above: Prior to 1968 drivers had wrestled with manual gearboxes and friction clutches, but early that year, to sighs of relief, SNOC/WNOC's first Bristol RELH6G/ECW 45-seater coaches (in Royal Blue livery but with Southern or Western National fleetnames) with semi-automatic gearboxes entered service. No 1450 (LDV 468F), was one of five to introduce semi-automatic transmission to WNOC's coach fleet, three similar examples doing likewise at SNOC. Later that same year a further eight such coaches (divided equally) joined the Royal Blue fleet. *G. F. Walker*

Above: At first glance it looks as though a brand-new Southdown Leyland Leopard/Plaxton 49-seater has been grabbed by a Royal Blue inspector as a last-minute relief vehicle and has parked beside a more usual WNOC Bristol — MW6G No 1390 (259 KTA) — at Salisbury coach station in July 1968. Not so; the Royal Blue timetable discloses that there was a 'joint' service with Southdown between Three Bridges (Crawley) and Totnes, Devon. In fact this was run solely by Southdown — and this was the Sunday coach to Totnes, which arrived in Salisbury at 12.47pm. *Mike Stephens*

Right: Feeder-service coach No 2205 (VDV 748), a Bristol LS6G/ECW 39-seater delivered to Western National in 1957, heads home to Helston with 'onward-transit' passengers collected at Paris Street coach station, Exeter. By then 11 years old, the vehicle had another two seasons to serve as a Royal Blue coach before going off in 1970 to join those of its batch which had found further employment with Morris Bros of Swansea. *Mike Stephens*

Right: Another Western National coach at a Southern National bus station. A Bristol MW6G with stepped-waistline ECW 39-seat bodywork dressed in Royal Blue livery awaits its turn to pick up passengers for a West Country tour starting at Newquay's Royal Blue coach station. The vehicle is No 1406 (744 MDV) of 1963 — equally available when required for upmarket private-hire work. *Mike Stephens*

Left: Setting out ex Paris Street coach station, Exeter, on a typical route-extension service frequently allotted to Southern or Western National coaches painted in Royal Blue livery is WNOC's No 1424 (EDV 506D), a Bristol MW6G/ECW 39-seater, new in 1966 — and, although a WNOC vehicle, originally ordered by Southern National. It was photographed about to head west for Liskeard and St Austell and the B3273 for Mevagissey Bay.
Mike Stephens

Left: Departing Exeter coach station in July 1968 for Honiton, Bridport and Bournemouth, via Hardy's Dorset, is Southern National's Royal Blue MW6G No 2277 (765 MDV), leaving behind a couple of Bristol coaches well-suited for use as weekend back-up vehicles for Royal Blue feeder services — or, indeed, journeys all the way to London Victoria.
The blasé gentleman with briefcase seems to have heard about the traditional reliability of a Royal Blue coach driver.
Mike Stephens

Right: March 1969, and Royal Blue drivers in need of passenger instructions gather around the much-liked 'Inspector Fred', in his famous wellies (worn rain or shine), beside the refreshment rooms at Yeovil Town station. On the left, Bristol MW6G/ ECW 39-seater No 2250 (617 DDV) of 1960 has arrived from Ilfracombe via Taunton and off-loaded its passengers, whilst Bristol RELH6G/ECW 45-seater No 2365 (HDV 624E) of 1967 has called in *en route* from Plymouth to London to provide the advertised connection. Both were the property of Southern National. *Mike Stephens*

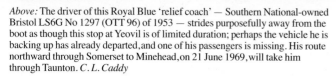

Above: The driver of this Royal Blue 'relief coach' — Southern National-owned Bristol LS6G No 1297 (OTT 96) of 1953 — strides purposefully away from the boot as though this stop at Yeovil is of limited duration; perhaps the vehicle he is backing up has already departed, and one of his passengers is missing. His route northward through Somerset to Minehead, on 21 June 1969, will take him through Taunton. *C. L. Caddy*

Above: Also at Yeovil on the same day, having completed a similar journey in the opposite direction, is sister vehicle No 1299 (OTT 98), displaying to advantage its nearside rear quarter. Five retractable steps rising between the two doors of the boot gave access, via grab-rails, to a curved slideway into the roof-mounted luggage pannier. Reaching this called for a fair degree of athleticism and nerve on the part of the driver, and none mourned its passing with this batch of 1953 coaches. *C. L. Caddy*

Left: Devon General AEC Regent double-deckers lurk above at Paris Street bus and coach station, Exeter, on 15 March 1970 as Bristol MW6G/ECW Royal Blue coach No 2262 (51 GUO) stands in splendid isolation below. It was more usual for Southern/Western National coaches (latterly in Royal Blue colours but with appropriate company fleetname) or hired-in examples from other operators to undertake 'relief work', but as more-elderly dedicated Royal Blue vehicles passed their prime, so too were they called upon.
C. L. Caddy

Right: Southern National colour contrast in Broad Street, Lyme Regis, in the autumn of 1969. Although neither of these two Bristol LS6G/ECW coaches is engaged upon express work, and their side elevations are now the same, the Royal Blue coach No 2212 (VDV 775) of 1957 at least retains the distinctive frontal destination screens of its predecessors. Compare with those featured upon the emerging No 1374 (OTT 83), still dressed in green and cream but dating from four years earlier.
DWR Picture Library

Prior to 1968 the Bristol RELH6G had been fitted with a manual gearbox, making the 20 delivered up to that year for Royal Blue service somewhat heavy to handle. The driver's task was eased considerably thereafter with the fitment of a semi-automatic alternative. So fitted, therefore, was No 1480 (RDV 431H), new in 1970 just after the demise of Southern National and allocated to Weymouth depot, where it was photographed in brand-new condition on 2 June that year. *C. L. Caddy*

On 20 December 1969 members of the Dorset Transport Circle paid a visit to Swindon to survey the transport scene in the town that gave birth to most of those fine steam locomotives which once graced the Great Western Railway. They had secured the services of Southern National's Weymouth-based Bristol MW6G No 1416 (EDV 546D) of 1966 with 39-seat ECW bodywork built to the third, most sophisticated, and final pattern produced for that chassis, at a time when the larger Bristol RE was already on stream.
C.L. Caddy

Among the more unusual destinations served by Royal Blue vehicles (and those in Royal Blue colours but with Southern or Western National fleetnames, for working those companies' share of the Associated Motorways network) were 'connection points' in the East Midlands. On 13 June 1970 driver Brian Jackson sets out from Weymouth with ex-SNOC Bristol MW6G No 1415 (EDV 545D), bound for Mansfield, Notts, on the regular summer Saturday service for points north.
C. L. Caddy

Left: Not too far to go for Totnes, yet mother looks perplexed and young daughter relies upon a Western National coach for support until the problem is solved. The vehicle, Bristol RELH6G/ ECW 45-seater No 1465 (OTA 637G) of 1969, was about to operate a local Royal Blue feeder service from Paris Street, Exeter, on 12 July 1970, by which time similar vehicles allotted to Southern National had been formally transferred into the WNOC fleet. *C. L. Caddy*

Left: Despite taking a rest at Exeter on 12 July 1970 in the company of a Royal Blue Bristol MW6G and a Southdown Leyland Leopard having its boot emptied, Bristol RELH6G No 1476 (RDV 427H) appears to have come up light from Plymouth after a run from London Victoria via Guildford, Winchester and points west. This vehicle was among several to carry the 'Mayflower 70' badge celebrating the 350th anniversary of that vessel's voyage from Plymouth to New England — even though it started at Greenwich and called at Southampton beforehand! *C. L. Caddy*

Right: Southern National's Bristol MW6G/ECW 39-seat coach No 1412 (EDV 542D), new in 1966, was one of numerous vehicles in both SNOC and WNOC fleets painted in Royal Blue livery so that intending passengers could identify them easily whilst they acted as express-service relief vehicles. Parked outside the refreshment rooms at Yeovil Town station on 2 August 1970, No 1412 was fully equipped for such work, having both 'ILFRACOMBE' and 'ROYAL BLUE' displayed in its destination apertures.
C. L. Caddy

Right: Taking a rest whilst *en route* from London Victoria to Plymouth via Exeter, No 2353 (839 SUO) stands beside W. H. Smith & Sons' warehouse in Yeovil on 2 August 1970. A Bristol RELH6G/ECW 45 seater new in 1964, it had been one of the first 14 REs to enter service with Royal Blue — 10 (including this one) for WNOC and four nominally the property of the Southern National Omnibus Co Ltd — but still had a further seven-and-a-bit years to serve before withdrawal.
C. L. Caddy

Left: Operating on behalf of Associated Motorways between Gloucester and Plymouth via Taunton and Exeter, Royal Blue Bristol MW6G/ECW 39-seater No 2238 (XUO 721), new to Western National in 1958, arrives in the city of Bristol, sweeping past a Bristol RELL/ECW saloon of the Bristol Omnibus Co Ltd. Years previously the latter company — as the Bristol Tramways & Carriage Co Ltd — had been a subsidiary of WNOC. *Mike Stephens*

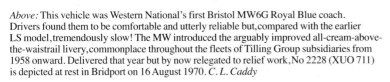

Above: This vehicle was Western National's first Bristol MW6G Royal Blue coach. Drivers found them to be comfortable and utterly reliable but, compared with the earlier LS model, tremendously slow! The MW introduced the arguably improved all-cream-above-the-waistrail livery, commonplace throughout the fleets of Tilling Group subsidiaries from 1958 onward. Delivered that year but by now relegated to relief work, No 2228 (XUO 711) is depicted at rest in Bridport on 16 August 1970. *C. L. Caddy*

Above: En route from Bournemouth to Ilfracombe in August 1970, Western National Bristol MW6G/ECW 39-seater No 2266 (55 GUO) of 1961 has called in for its refreshment stop at Yeovil Town station, built for the GWR in 1860. As a temporary companion No 2266 has a more youthful vehicle in the livery of Southern National/Royal Blue — applied specifically to aid recognition when used on express-service relief work. *C. L. Caddy*

Right: In 1968 SNOC took
delivery of seven Bristol
RELH6G/ECW 45-seater
coaches, of which only four
were actually labelled
'Royal Blue'. 'Southern National'
No 1456 (LDV 466F) and its
two fellows were nevertheless
painted in Royal Blue colours
ready to undertake express
duties when so required.
It was photographed at Weymouth
on 4 November 1970 —
by which time it was legally
a Western National vehicle!
C. L. Caddy

Right: Delivered in 1966 with
the latter-day ECW bodywork
for the Bristol MW — which
remained in production
following the introduction
of the RE — was MW6G
No 1421 (EDV 503D), the first
of nine for Western National.
At Exeter's Paris Street coach
station on 7 August 1971,
it was bound for Plymouth and
promising connections beyond
for Cornwall. A window sticker
states bizarrely that it is on hire
to Western National.
C. L. Caddy

Left: Despite the rather ominous information 'Terminal Blind No 12' in the upper destination aperture and the red sticker in the windscreen, this coach — photographed at Rutland Road Works, Bournemouth, on 13 May 1973 — has not yet been condemned to withdrawal. Bristol MW6G/ECW 39-seater No 2246 (625 DDV), new to Western National in 1960, duly responded to remedial action and would put in another two years' service, ultimately being sold for further use as school transport in Cornwall. *C. L. Caddy*

Left: A Western National driver admires the fast-disappearing traditional 'Royal Blue' image at Yeovil on 3 June 1973. Looking very smart but with just days to go before withdrawal, Bristol MW6G No 2249 (616 DDV) — new to Southern National in 1960 — prepares to set off for the north coast of Somerset and the 'Lorna Doone' country of Exmoor *en route* to Ilfracombe in Devon. Notwithstanding the vehicle's age, this was one of the most strenuous routes in the entire Royal Blue network. *C. L. Caddy*

Not too long after the National Bus Company came into being its board of directors began to consider a corporate image for its vehicles. Initially what turned out to be an interim scheme for the coaches of its subsidiaries in the South West was devised, comprising a white base with a coloured waistband recalling the respective operations' original identity. Looking somewhat sheepish in white with just a thin dark-blue band, 'Royal Blue' Bristol MW6G No 2276 (764 MDV) of 1963 exits Bournemouth Coach Station in July 1970. *W. T. Cansick*

Throughout the 'Sixties few could have guessed that the days of dark-blue-and-cream Royal Blue express coaches bustling along 'A'-class roads, making intermittent detours into a village to pick up or set down beside the local Royal Blue booking office, were coming to an end. For posterity's sake it is worth recording how Clement Preece's staff used to advertise the joys of that mode of travel, as against, in contrast, what the railway had to offer — each town and village viewed in 'rear close-up', tatty garden sheds, washing on the clothes lines and curious examples of individual taste in very quick succession:

'The luxuriously-appointed long-distance coaches operate from Victoria Coach Station in London, which is equipped with waiting rooms and every up-to-date convenience for the use of passengers and their luggage. So comfortable and commodious are the Royal Blue coaches that the 250 to 300 miles journey between London and Cornwall can be accomplished without any undue fatigue and with fullest enjoyment of the ever-changing scenery through which the route passes.

'London is left by the Great West Road, passing through Staines, Egham and Bagshot. Then on past Basingstoke to Andover and the wide expanse of Salisbury Plain. After leaving the cathedral city of Wiltshire, the route touches Dorset, through the lovely old towns of Shaftesbury and Sherborne, and thence on to Yeovil in Somerset.

'Soon the lush Devonshire countryside is reached with Honiton, and so on to the ancient city of Exeter with its magnificent cathedral, Guildhall and mediaeval houses and churches which suffered such irreparable damage in the war.

'Over the [River] Exe the picturesque road goes on to Okehampton, skirting the northern fringe of Dartmoor with Cawsand Beacon, 1,799 feet above sea level, dominating the landscape. Thence the route bears south, passing near to Yes Tor and High Willhays, both of well over 2,000 feet elevation. After Lifton the road drops to cross the lovely Tamar Valley, which here defines the boundary between Devonshire and the duchy.

'Then up again, steeply into Launceston, the first and one of the most ancient of Cornish towns. From here the route traverses the moors to the county town of Bodmin, and thence on to Truro where passengers change coaches for Falmouth. The route proceeds through Camborne to Penzance with a connection at St. Erth for St. Ives.

'The company's Royal Blue timetable gives full details of journey times and stopping-places en route for refreshments.'

This little essay would not have won any prizes for literary merit, but it was written with justifiable pride. Proud also were the Royal Blue drivers whom managers and thousands of passengers considered the 'salt of the earth'. The advance of the nation's motorway system, politics and sheer economics were among the factors which were now set to alter the entire scenario of express coach operations. The personal reminiscences about and during this period of change are, unless otherwise stated, those of Howard Evans, Philip Emond and Alan Walker.

Following the Transport Act 1968 the road-transport interests of British Electric Traction had been brought into the nationalised fold of the Transport Holding Co This cleared the way for the formation of the National Bus Company ('national' in this instance meaning Government-owned) with effect from 1 January 1969. In line with NBC's policy on the subject of Excursions & Tours

business in general, both Southern and Western National began selling off that kind of coach operation to nearby local firms. By the end of that year Southern National and its operations had been transferred to Western National. From now on all Royal Blue coaches became the property of the latter. Prior to that there had always been efforts to 'return' each company's Royal Blue vehicle to its proper owner whenever convenient. 'As Royal Blue drivers we knew the difference: the little winged wheel on the sides of the earlier models told us if it was one of ours or not.' And then (curiously, as the Western company actually enjoyed a loan from Southern National extending over many years, and which it never actually repaid): 'There was always a bit of animosity between Southern and Western National. The Southern were always seen as "the scroungers".' If such were the feeling among stage-carriage crews, the Royal Blue crews got on well together regardless.

'When you got to Victoria, you unloaded in the coach station, then took the vehicle around to "Sammy's" [the Samuelson's garage, in Eccleston Place], where it would be washed and fuelled up. If you were lucky you then found somewhere nearby to park, but sometimes [you] had to go out a long way. In the former instance there was a visit then to "Bay 19" at Victoria — The Imperial in Eccleston Place, right opposite the exit. That's where all the "lucky" drivers would finish up when they'd arrived for an overnight stop — 15 or so coaches coming up from the West Country. All the tips we got were pooled. We'd buy one drink each out of it, and the rest of the money we'd split between us. Mind you, we had one or two drivers with short pockets; they'd only have about one and sixpence [7½p].'

'However, if you were unlucky and had to drive around looking for somewhere to park you could, say, get into Victoria at 9.17pm and very often didn't get back to the digs until 11 or 11.30pm. The temptation then was to use the "Royal Blue Hotel" — a "kip" on the back seat of your coach, which was strictly against company rules. Overnight accommodation was always a problem. You got 17/6 [87½p] per day subsistence — that was for bed and breakfast and whatever meals you needed to pay for' (which is why the 'perks' which drivers enjoyed at the various 'comfort stops' were such a help to them).

'I came in for duty one day and got hauled over the coals: "We've had a complaint that you've been sleeping on the back of the coach." Jack Gleeson took the enquiry. "OK, would you like to sleep in a very small room with five beds in it — no shower and lucky if you got a washbasin — and at two o'clock in the morning four non-drivers from points elsewhere come in the worse for drink and create mayhem? If you sleep on the back seat and in the morning go over and have a shower in the drivers' room at Victoria Coach Station you're in a proper shape to drive a coach-load back to the West Country." Gleeson agreed!

'What I could never understand was why Royal Blue insisted on West Country-based drivers going all the way up to London. Why not change over halfway? A London-based driver (and there were plenty of them) going, say, as far as Yeovil could have got back home every night, and, conversely, so could we.'

An early decision by NBC as to what to do with the image of its coach services was to oblige its subsidiaries at Bristol and in the West Country to adopt a new livery. Henceforward existing coaches and new intakes were to be white with a fleet-identifying coloured waistband. For Bristol Greyhound, which had hitherto employed cream with a bright-red band, magenta was the choice; Black & White, not unnaturally, chose black, Greenslades a bluish green, and Devon General's 'Grey Cars' grey. In what turned out to be merely a stay of execution for their traditional hue, Western National's coaches were given a waistband of royal blue, though just how much royal blue depended upon the depth of each coach's 'waist'. The fleets involved in this exercise were afterward gathered into a marketing project for services from the West to London. New vehicles delivered with the royal-blue band in the years 1970-3 were Bristol LHs bodied by Duple, Plaxton or Marshall and Bristol RELHs with 47-seat Plaxton coachwork. Other vehicles to wear this livery style were half a dozen 7ft 6in-wide AEC Reliance/Willowbrook coaches new as Devon General 'Grey Cars' but acquired from the associated Greenslades fleet, principally to work Royal Blue 'feeder' services.

Some British Railways official with no sense of history has ordered 'SOUTHERN RAILWAY' to be obliterated on the 'Private Road' sign as a Royal Blue coach until very recently owned by Southern National pulls away from the Yeovil Town refreshment stop. Now officially a Western National vehicle, No 1408 (757 MDV), a Bristol MW6G/ECW 39-seater of 1963, presents a mildly startling appearance in South West area livery on 16 August 1970.
C. L. Caddy

Above: Associated Motorways shared the cosy little wooden office at Bridport with Royal Blue, but on this occasion — on 17 February 1973 — No 2379 (OTA 639G) has called in on the latter's behalf. Wearing the short-lived South Western area livery, the vehicle is a Bristol RELH6G with 45-seat ECW coachwork; offering 'connections for Cornwall', it was bound for Exeter and the 'deviation' terminus of Kingsbridge, on the South Hams peninsula.
C. L. Caddy

Right: If the new livery of dark blue and white did anything to enhance Royal Blue's Bristol REs it certainly made them look considerably longer than before. The effect is quite marked in this three-quarter rear view of No 2378 (LDV 850F), new in 1968 but photographed — at Victoria — in August 1971. An unexpected effect of all that white was that it picked out in stark relief every panel, hinge, air-intake etc — as well as needing a lot more washing. *W. T. Cansick*

Left: Surprisingly it was those vehicles bodied by Eastern Coach Works which came off worst in the Royal Blue version of the South Western area livery, the bodywork mouldings in each case dictating a shallow waistband. The dozen Bristol LH6L coaches bodied by Duple looked the better for their deeper band of dark blue — even if the expanse of chromium beneath looked a little garish. No 1309 (RDV 444H) demonstrates at Victoria in July 1971. *W. T. Cansick*

Below: In a similar vein, the first seven Royal Blue coaches to be bodied by Plaxton — Bristol RELH6Gs delivered in 1971 — also benefited from a broader band of dark blue. Like its six fellows a 47-seater, No 2394 (UTT 563J) was photographed in May 1971 in the temporary care of the Bristol Omnibus Co, whilst in the course of delivery from Plaxton's Scarborough factory to Western National's Plymouth depot. *D. Withers*

Above left: Surprisingly the vehicles left looking most like their forebears were the ex-Devon General AEC Reliance/Willowbrook 41-seaters which came into the Royal Blue fleet via Greenslades Tours of Exeter in 1970/1. Although primarily used by Western National on Devon tours, they frequently turned up on Royal Blue 'express-extension' services which needed to negotiate the narrower byways of the West Country. At 7ft 6in wide these vehicles — among them No 1240 (937 GTA) — were ideal for the task. *Ian Allan Library*

Right: Delivered in 1970 were a dozen Leyland-engined Bristol LH6Ls with 41-seat Duple coachwork to a design offering all-round vision not experienced since the days of the open charabanc. Wending its way through Yeovil when but a few weeks old, No 1304 (RDV 439H) displays the South Western area version of Royal Blue livery while *en route* from Bournemouth to Minehead via Taunton on service X18. *C. L. Caddy*

Right: Allocated to Weymouth from new for both private-hire and Royal Blue express-relief work, Bristol LH6L/Duple 41-seater No 1309 (RDV 444H) was photographed on 4 July 1970 in the company of a Black & White coach at the local Radipole garage of Western National — appropriate, for this was one of the last vehicles to have been ordered from the manufacturers by the Southern National Omnibus Co Ltd. *C. L. Caddy*

Left: Loading satisfactorily at Paris Street, Exeter on 7 August 1971 is newly-delivered Bristol RELH6G No 2398 (UTT 567J), one of an initial batch fitted with 47-seat Plaxton coachwork. Wearing South Western area livery in the days before NBC imposed its 'all-white coach' policy upon its subsidiary companies, No 2398 has been selected to operate to Cheltenham as part of Royal Blue's contribution to the Associated Motorways network. *C. L. Caddy*

Left: A particularly rare bird, being one of just four of this chassis/body combination built for Royal Blue service, was No 1315 (UTT 581J), a Bristol LH6L/Plaxton 41-seater, captured by the camera at Exeter's Paris Street coach station on 7 August 1971, when newly delivered. The last few passengers for Bournemouth seem satisfied that their luggage has been properly loaded into the boot prior to departure. *C. L. Caddy*

The last batch of Royal Blue coaches to be delivered new with even a trace of dark blue arrived in 1973, this doubtful privilege being enjoyed by 10 Bristol LH6L 39-seater coaches bodied by Marshall of Cambridge (Engineering) Ltd. The coachbuilder nevertheless made up for the curtailment of the blue band at the rear by painting the lower front panel blue instead. When photographed in August 1974 No 1323 (NTT 323M) was set to run to Barnstaple on National Express 710 from Victoria. *W. T. Cansick*

Upon his appointment as Chairman of NBC, Freddie (later Sir Frederick) Wood took a long, hard look at coach operations in particular — and became convinced that the travelling public were 'confused' by all the differing liveries worn by express coaches heading for Cheltenham, London and other exchange points or termini. Probably influenced by the nationwide network of services operated in the United States by Greyhound Coach Lines, he opted for a unified 'National' image. All coaches of NBC's subsidiaries employed upon express services or extended tours were to be placed into a 'National Travel' division; all were to be painted white, with a large '**NATIONAL**' logo in alternate red and blue lettering. Individual fleet origins were indicated above the front wheel-arches, initially in grey with an underlining in the traditional colour, so that, for a while, at least, that thin strip of paint was all that remained of the famous Royal Blue hue. There were second thoughts, however, at NBC, the thin blue strip being seen as a threat to the holistic new image being sought. It was duly removed, and all participant-company identities were instead replaced, irrespective of origin, in red. Thereafter all-white 'Royal Blue' coaches were labelled as such in red!

There was arguably a flaw or two attached to the desire for this 'white as snow' image designed principally for ready recognition whilst out on service upon the road. Finding one's coach at an express-service exchange-point such as Salisbury or Exeter, where vehicles were not parked with a clearly identified route indicator above (as was the case at Victoria or Cheltenham) had traditionally been made that much easier by being able to say 'There's our green Southdown / rufous Midland Red / pied Black & White over there' in the way that we look for clues as to how we find our car in a large parking lot. Secondly, when traffic was at its busiest, during the traditional weekend surge, it still remained necessary to hire in all those independently owned multi-coloured vehicles as duplicates, which continued to cause uncertainty in identification at stops along each route. As late as 1975, for instance, it was not unusual to find a red Princess-Summerbee from Southampton turning up at Worthing as an express relief to Brighton's Pool Valley — or, in circumstances not too extreme,

a prosaic Leyland National performing the same task elsewhere as a last-minute stand-in, dressed in leaf green. NBC's bright-new-pin image became unfastened somewhat at such times.

'The business of grabbing hold of any vehicles to get the passengers to London or anywhere else, particularly on Saturdays, continued apace. Well, yes, I've done it with Bristol RE saloon buses — Nos 2715 and 2719 — and anything else that was available, whether it was white, blue, green or whatever. That was commonplace even in the early days at Taunton when we got the railway-replacement contract from Taunton up to Bristol. There were three coaches on that contract, and we used to get a nice four- or five-hour stand-by in Bristol. But then they decided that was a waste of valuable time, so they'd send us through to London and back. Sometimes we didn't get back to Bristol in time to do the return contract trip. You left about 7.15 in the morning and didn't get back 'til about 6.30 in the evening — quite a long day. And, of course, in the evening, instead of doing a local service in Bristol, you could be sent back to Heathrow Airport or London. Very often, if the M4 was bad, you had to phone the depot and, because there were no mobile phones in those days, had to pull in somewhere like Leigh Delamere Services in Wiltshire to warn the inspector in Taunton. He then had to scramble a bus from Taunton to fulfil the railway-replacement contract requirement.'

Left: Probably the most box-like bodywork ever fitted to Royal Blue coaches was that built on 10 Bristol LH6L chassis by Marshall of Cambridge in 1973; these were also the last vehicles delivered in the blue-and-white South Western area livery. Taking a rest from its touring duties based upon Exeter, No 1324 (NTT 324M) was photographed on 16 April 1974, prior to being rendered even more stark by a repaint in overall white. *C. L. Caddy*

Below left: From 1973 all new coaches for Royal Blue express services were delivered in overall white. At first the fleetname was carried in small grey letters (over the front wheel arch) underlined in blue to emphasise fleet origin, but the 'double N' and '**NATIONAL**' in large alternate red/blue letters now showed who was boss. Probably because of their close-panelled finish, body styling and larger windows — or just sheer familiarity — more-modern coaches looked better suited to their minimalist livery. However, those of us who have temporarily 'lost' our car in a car park will agree with the photographer, who writes: 'Imagine Exeter Coach Station full of similar vehicles in identical livery and only very small fleetnames …' How apt; Plaxton-bodied Bristol RELH6G 47-seater No 2393 illustrates both points in August 1972. *Graham Hadley*

Right: Soon even the thin blue line beneath the fleetname disappeared. Bristol MW6G No 1438 (HDV 621E) of 1967, with latter-day style of ECW coach bodywork for this chassis type, looks nowhere near as attractive as it was when new: the application of white overall has served to emphasise each panel and fitment. At least the vehicle would have been visually unmissable as it motored up to town from Combe Martin and Ilfracombe in August 1975. Having set down his passengers at Victoria Coach Station, the driver — in time-honoured fashion — is reversing into an overnight parking spot in a nearby street. *W. T. Cansick*

Right: New in 1970, this Bristol LH6L/Duple express-service coach has recently received the whitewash treatment — with Royal Blue name now in red (!) — and one has the impression that, had it proven feasible, the radiator grille, bumper and even the chromium band would have been overpainted white. No 1306 (RDV 441H) is parked beside the hedge planted by Elliott Bros, many decades previously, beside the works in Rutland Road, Bournemouth. *John Robinson*

Left: So handsome in their original livery, Royal Blue's Bristol RELH6G/ECW coaches lost much of their *élan* when painted in National white. No 1460 (OTA 632G) of 1969 looks positively ghostly at Bedford Place coach station, Southampton. *Ian Allan Library*

The weekend express-services rush continued to be a nerve-wracking time for Royal Blue inspectors or other officers entrusted with the task of successfully getting from A to B all those passengers who descended, sometimes unexpectedly, upon their personal patch. The most unlikely solutions were sometimes employed. Miss Veronica Gunn MBE, the legendary proprietress of Safeway Services, South Petherton, recalled (1982): 'We had a nice new 43-seater coach. My manager used to drive it down to Weymouth on day tours and they [Royal Blue] would ask if in the interim we would back them up to Bournemouth. Well, that was not too bad, but when he got there an inspector would say: "Right, London!" "No way," he'd reply; "I've got a party down at Weymouth to get back to Somerset." "Oh dear! Weymouth told me you'd go through to London for us." One Saturday he unloaded in Bournemouth, and they said: "We don't know what to do with all these crowds of people here, they're milling about the station. Will you run them down to Taunton for us?" He realised he'd have time to spare to do that, so he agreed. Well, when he got down to Taunton, these people refused to get off my coach! They said: "We've travelled from the other side of London, and this is the fourth coach we've been in, and now we're expected to get in another one to reach Ilfracombe?" Our driver came back and said: "Don't take on any more jobs like that: it was terrible what I had to put up with from those people." He had all that harassment — and I've never done anything for them since!'

As the motorways extended ever southward and westward, so the express routes and timetables were altered to reflect the changing needs of passengers. Travelling in relatively leisurely fashion, taking in numerous idyllic villages along the way, was replaced by schedules designed to get the 'customers' to their destinations as quickly as possible. Previously restricted by law to a maximum speed of 50mph on 'A'-class roads, Royal Blue coaches (and all others) using the motorways were now able to take advantage of the appropriate regulations and go faster. The now elderly and 'geared-down' Bristol MWs were phased out of service and replaced with numerous Leyland Leopards fitted, in the main, with Plaxton coachwork.

To a certain extent the Royal Blue waistband and front dash on the Marshall-bodied Bristol LH coaches helped mask severe rectilinear lines when they were delivered in 1973. When, subsequently, they were repainted in overall white, all was revealed; their shape would clearly have made an ideal model for a presentation biscuit tin. No 1317 (NTT 317M), *en route* from Ilfracombe to Bournemouth, was photographed scurrying through Poole on 28 May 1975. *John Robinson*

One unexpected and fascinating result of these higher speeds provided drivers so inclined with the opportunity to undertake a little nature study and wonder at the canny adaptability of wildlife: 'One of the things we used to see at Victoria Coach Station in summertime, after flying down the motorway, collecting lots of dead flies on the front, was that all the house sparrows in the neighbourhood would come down and clean off the windscreens for you by actually hovering in front of the glass or standing on the wiper blades. And they'd eat all the dead flies off the windows — no fee! It amazed me that these sparrows could hold there and actually flutter whilst they were doing it. They used to sit up in the rafters waiting for the next coach to come in and stop — then they'd all swoop down and do their vacuuming. Occasionally you'd get some help in that regard from a few wasps which did the same thing.'

The Leyland Leopards employed on these express services included some equipped with a twin-speed high- and low-ratio capabilty. The drivers tended to call them 'twin-axle' Leopards. 'You flicked a switch and it went up or down. I don't know how it worked mechanically, but it was on the back wheels. When I was in Dagenham, I learned how to drive one before I came down to the West Country. When I arrived in Taunton nobody believed I knew how to drive a "twin-axle", so I was given a road test in one. I only went a few

hundred yards up the road and was asked to return. The inspector said: "Yup, he knows how to drive it!"

Meanwhile the Bristol REs, which never looked so good in National white livery, were approaching their sell-by date. One of the services upon which they continued to labour was the South Coast Express, which an East Kent driver would take over at Brighton and pilot through to Ramsgate. 'On frequent occasions these REs broke down — they were getting to the end of their lives … because one of them broke down in Eastbourne, this gentleman here brought me back a Southdown Ford one night which had a horrible back-to-front gearbox. [Actually it was the close-together six gates of the gears which made them difficult to engage in the correct order.] Sometimes you'd get into Brighton ready to come back and find yourself in charge of a six-speed AEC from East Kent to take to Bournemouth or even Taunton.'

In July 1976 came the fire at the famous Bournemouth Bus & Coach Station in The Square, which effectively ended the role of that location as the centre of Royal Blue operations. For some 10 months afterward Royal Blue's services in Bournemouth began or terminated at the Holdenhurst Road depot of Shamrock & Rambler. Thereafter the operational centres of Royal Blue were withdrawn to the West Country. With the demise of Bournemouth Coach Station so too disappeared the time-honoured title of TSRB (Traffic Superintendent, Royal Blue) Bournemouth.

The days of Cheltenham Coach Station and its famous mass departures were also numbered, as NBC sought to cut costs and find alternative 'centres of gravity' for its express services. What had been the 4pm departure was brought forward to 3pm or thereabouts because it was taking longer to reach destinations on the second leg. 'Cheltenham was a major interchange. When you looked at it on a map it looked quite a way south, but it was like the centre of a spider's web — a stroke of genius, really; all interchanges took place there. Services coming up from the south and west exchanged passengers for all points north and into Wales. The most busy time I remember was when a big national rail strike was on; there were duplicates and triplicates coming in from all directions. I came up to Cheltenham along the dual-carriageway and went left up a side street under a railway bridge about half a mile from the coach station. I joined the queue to enter under that bridge — and about an hour and a half later got to the coach station. Once there they unloaded us very, very slowly and tried to keep the drivers to a minimum possible break. We loaded up as and when it was possible to leave the station — if, that was, you could actually get out. It was just a continuous line of coaches. One rather nice run which was still operating in those days was from Portsmouth to Southampton, Salisbury, Collingbourne Ducis (one

In 1980 National Bus Company officials celebrated the '100th anniversary of Royal Blue' by hiring a coach-and-four from Dodington Coach Museum in Gloucestershire and staging an 'anniversary run' from Holmsley railway station to the Royal Bath Hotel at Bournemouth. A very nice day out, but sadly (as explained earlier) neither date nor route were entirely appropriate. However, to mark the date when, in fact, Thomas Elliott obtained his first licence to drive a cab, numerous Leyland Leopard coaches wore a 'centenary sticker' — including Plaxton-bodied No 2444 (SFJ 144R) of 1977. *G. K. Gillberry*

driver did go via Pewsey once but wasn't meant to — I'd shown him the way, but he got it wrong), Marlborough, Swindon and Cirencester to Cheltenham. Then they stopped using Cheltenham Coach Station, and everything was split between Birmingham and Bristol — and exactly the same thing happened in Bristol. Not long after the Cheltenham closure we were queuing up on the dual-carriageway in the centre to get into that coach station — and "Uncle Bill" was going up the wall. The same thing happened in Birmingham.'

'Howard was talking about being grabbed to go anywhere: one summer Saturday I turned up at Bristol and was queuing to get in when the manager there, Trevor Smallbone, came out and said: "You're just the guy I want!" I said: "I can't do anything — I've got to go to Bath." He said: "Well, if I take your passengers and make sure they get to Bath, will you do me a favour? I need a coach to go to North Devon and Ilfracombe, and you're the only driver I've seen who will know which way to go." So I 'phoned Taunton, and Inspector Chittenden gave his approval. Next morning I had an early breakfast, and when I came back the coach was already loaded. It was down virtually non-stop to Minehead and every blade of grass from there — over the top, not via Porlock but up through Dunster and down through Wheddon Cross,

and on to Ilfracombe. It was the most stunning day you ever could have wished, and I shall always remember it. That was a most fantastic journey, and it was somewhere I never expected to be that day.'

'They'd grab you for anywhere if they could. I remember on one occasion in London they wanted me to go up north, which would have meant an overnight stay, but I declined because I had no overnight bag with me. They'd try anything to keep the passengers moving. The X96 to Bath alternated with a journey instead to Cardiff. At one stage an ordinary Leyland National saloon bus was substituted for a trip to Cardiff — just an ordinary bus! You had to work twice as hard on that: it had power steering, but if you let go of the steering wheel you had to heave it back to where you wanted it.'

'We also had three comparatively old Leyland Leopards on the Taunton–Bristol rail-replacement service, and they were very heavy to drive because they had no power steering on them. That was OK if you were going up to London, but for a six-month period we ended up going all the way from London through to Dulverton and down to Minehead and all around Watchet, through winding, twisty roads — and you really knew you'd done a day's work when you'd finished driving that one! I once did that trip with a Dennis Falcon.'

Right: The prototype for this Leyland Leopard/Willowbrook 003 combination having been delivered to Western National the previous year, the remainder of the 10-strong batch arrived in 1980, among them No 3533 (FDV 824V). Intended primarily for Royal Blue express work, they were nevertheless completed as 'grant coaches', with folding doors facilitating their employment on stage-carriage services (and offering the operator a tax concession upon the purchase cost). *Ian Allan Library*

Below: Faced with increased competition from the private sector in the wake of the Transport Act 1980, NBC raised its game by ordering higher-specification rolling stock. 'So nearly Royal Blue coaches' were five Dennis Falcon V/Duple Goldliner 47-seaters delivered in the autumn of 1982, by which time WNOC had abandoned use of this illustrious fleetname. Pictured departing Victoria for Plymouth in November of that year, No 2352 (AOD 645Y) was thus branded '**WESTERN NATIONAL**'; the '*Rapide*' brand, applied to longer-distance services, was adopted by National Express following a tie-up with erstwhile competitor Trathens of Yelverton, which operator's fleetname is superimposed amidships. *L. Lennox*

The Dennis Falcon V, with Perkins V8 engine and Duple Goldliner bodywork, was produced specifically for National Express 'Rapide' services. Of the 10 built, five were allocated for Royal Blue service, although by the time they arrived, in the autumn of 1982, this time-honoured fleetname was being phased out, and they entered service as 'Western National' vehicles. Deprived of a proper opportunity to put its new type through what would have been a full regime of testing (because of pressure from NBC to deliver them as soon as possible), Dennis saw its reputation unfairly tested. Yet those who drove it thought the Falcon a potential prizewinner. 'They were the fastest coaches I ever drove. You used to be able to pull out of Battersea Coach Park and you could accelerate faster away from the lights with those than anything else I ever had. But they had this tendency to lose power when least expected. I had to take one up to Dennis at Guildford on one occasion, and it took me practically all day to get there. Not surprisingly, Dennis asked what was wrong. Apparently everything had filters, just like the very same engines they put in fire engines. But fire engines are serviced practically every day; our coaches weren't. So, in the end, the more filters they took off, the more reliable the Falcons became. But they were fantastic vehicles to drive — the noisiest thing about them, from what I can remember, was the wind whistling through the wing mirrors.'

Needless to say, Dennis survived this episode and today represents the best of British manufacturing skills. Following on from several examples of drivers' visual acuity, the next reminiscence serves to highlight also their audio-perceptual sharpness. It was always there: 'I think that the Bedford OB was one of the prettiest coaches there ever was. The distinctive note of the gearbox was absolutely wonderful. Whenever I drove one, I used deliberately to change down a gear just to listen to it. But then I used to do that coming up out of Watchet with a Bristol RE; I'd come alongside a wall, drop a gear, open a window and listen to that lovely noise. Same with the Leyland Leopard — and in ordinary bus work also, even the Bristol VR double-deckers, if you knew where to do it; favourite place for me was beneath the railway-station bridge in Taunton — the racket that came through that window was brilliant.'

Left: After the disastrous fire at Bournemouth bus and coach station in July 1976 Royal Blue departures and arrivals from/at that resort returned once again to Holdenhurst Road — after a 45-year absence. Ten months later the Royal Blue fleet was withdrawn to points west, centred upon Exeter and Plymouth. National Express then 'hired in' the competing Trathens of Yelverton, which subsequently ran its non-stop Plymouth–London service with coaches dressed in National white and bearing both Trathens and Royal Blue fleetnames. Here Trathens' Volvo B10M/ Berkhof No 64 (BDV 864Y) enters Victoria Coach Station on 22 June 1983. *M. S. Stokes*

After the Western National Omnibus Co Ltd was split into four operational units with effect from 1 January 1983, only that part which became the new Western National Ltd chose to retain the 'Royal Blue' name upon its coaches, express or otherwise. Under the new regime just two further vehicular types would be added to the roster of Royal Blue coaches. The first was the Leyland Tiger with 46-seat Plaxton Paramount coachwork, to be joined later by a pair of similarly seated examples bodied by Duple. And the last new type to operate on the core 'Rapide' route between Plymouth and London Victoria was a double-decker. Of the eight integral MCW Metroliner coaches delivered to Western National Ltd, just the first four bore 'Royal Blue' — in red. In 1986 the firm decided to abandon the famous name, although it lingered on a few more years upon blue-painted 'local coach' vehicles in Cornwall. Surprisingly, however, the last coach to take the road in traditional colours and with Royal Blue fleetnames was a Bristol RELH/ECW coach which operated a Taunton–Bournemouth express service and was introduced as a last hurrah by the now privatised Southern National Ltd in 1992 (and illustrated in *Glory Days: Royal Blue*).

Of the three express-coach drivers whose testimony forms the basis of this chapter, it is perhaps appropriate to give the final words to the senior member of the group. 'It wasn't a question of working in a factory from nine 'til six; you did the job because you liked it — and there was plenty of overtime, or people wouldn't have stuck it for 40 years. You're not going to get them doing it now for 40 years, because the working regime is nowhere near as companionable. I've been on for 41 years, and up until recently we had a lot of long-service drivers, but there aren't going to be so many in the future, because nobody's got a job for life in any profession. When I was at Bude I was the youngest driver they had there, and the driver next-senior to me was a 25-year man. Those days are gone.'

So said Howard Evans, who, like the other two witnesses for this chapter, drove upon Royal Blue routes both old and more (comparatively) recent and rose to a more senior rank within the profession. Thank you to them, to those who unfolded their tales of the days with Royal Blue in earlier decades, and to those whose names I never knew who drove with such style the Royal Blue coaches I was so glad to travel in to Bournemouth and the blessed West Country from 1940 onwards. Happy Royal Blue days indeed!

Right: By 1982 coaches in the reduced Royal Blue fleet specifically dedicated to National Express work bore the marketing name 'Rapide', derived from the tie-up with Trathens. As a nod toward recompense for the withdrawal from Bournemouth, Royal Blue vehicles were now employed far and wide. Still in familiar territory, however, on 28 December 1983, was Western National Ltd's No 2203 (A749 VAF), a Leyland Tiger with Plaxton Paramount 3500 bodywork, diverted from Midland Red, the photographer bravely recording its presence at Digbeth despite that day's bomb alert. *M. Bott*

Right: After the Western National Omnibus Co Ltd was divided into four separate companies only the new Western National Ltd decided to retain the Royal Blue fleetname. As NBC's corporate image was relaxed so its subsidiaries nationwide began to apply a little more traditional colour to their vehicles; in 1984 Leopard/Plaxton 'grant coach' No 3549 (FDV 805V) of 1980 emerged in this version of what was soon nicknamed 'venetian blind' livery, comprising a blue band and diagonal with red stripes superimposed thereon. *Ian Allan Library*

As the National Bus Company began to loosen its hold, so its subsidiary companies seized the opportunity to replace some colour on their 'whitewashed' express coaches. The new Western National Ltd jumped at the chance to put some royal blue back where it belonged — and briefly applied red as well. Leyland Leopard/Plaxton No 3542 (FDV 798V) of 1980 still wore this livery when photographed at Weymouth on 11 June 1983. *C. L. Caddy*

Right: Western National Ltd operated eight integral MCW Metroliner double-deck coaches on the National Express 'Rapide' service between Plymouth and London Victoria. Shadowed by a Trathens DAF/Jonckheere of similar configuration, WN No 1404 (A759 VAF) prepares to depart Breton Side bus station in August 1984. This was one of just four Metroliners to display the Royal Blue name (twice upon each side, but in red) before it was dropped — officially from 1986. *Adrian A. Thomas*

Left: By 1984 the blue, red and white Royal Blues of Western National Ltd were largely employed on upmarket tours from Plymouth. The welcoming warmth of the red 'venetian-blind' stripes was now supplemented by red curtains at the windows, whilst a black skirt all-round created the impression of greater length, beyond the 12m maximum to which most coaches were now being built. With retractable step lowered, No 2208 (A532 WRL), a Leyland Tiger with 46-seat Plaxton Paramount 3200 coachwork, awaits further tourists at Plymouth's Breton Side bus station on 30 August 1984. *Adrian A. Thomas*

Left: When the Royal Blue fleetname was finally removed from Western National's main express routes between London and Plymouth, Penzance etc it was replaced by 'CORNWALL COACHWAYS' in 'not so' easy to read style. The latter was applied both to 'Rapide' coaches and — in more overt fashion — to 'onward transit' vehicles. Into the latter category fell WN No 2430 (GTA 811N), a one-time 'Royal Blue' Leyland Leopard/Plaxton 47-seater of 1975, photographed at Breton Side bus station on 10 May 1984. *A. Swain*

Right: Its retention, as late as 1988, of the Royal Blue title upon the flanks of a few Plaxton-bodied Leopards running about in Cornwall suggested that WN was in two minds as to whether to let go of such a tried and trusted name. The same might be said of its use in that county of coach-seated double-deckers in National Express white livery but also labelled '**WESTERN NATIONAL**'. Leyland Olympian/ECW 'coach' No 1807 (A754 VAF), new in 1984, sounds the knell of parting days at Truro bus station *en route* from Plymouth to Penzance in April 1986. *Adrian A. Thomas*

TAILPIECE

Chassis makes and models of vehicles that bore the Royal Blue fleetname between 1913 and 1986, listed in order of entry into service

Vehicles in the two left-hand columns entered service in Elliott Bros ownership, the remainder under Tilling, BTC, THC or NBC control.

Dennis 3-ton	AEC Reliance	Bristol JJW	Leyland Tiger Cub *
Daimler CC	Daimler CF6	Leyland Tiger TS3	Bristol RELH6G
Selden 30-40hp	AEC Regal	Leyland Tiger TS1	Bristol RELH6L
De Dion Bouton	Maudslay ML6	Bristol L6B	Bristol LH6L
AEC YC	Leyland Tiger TS2	Bristol L6A	AEC Reliance
Daimler CK	Gilford 168OT	Bristol LL6B	Leyland Leopard
Daimler Y	Chevrolet U	Bristol LS6G	Leyland Tiger
Crossley X	Dennis Lancet	Bedford OB	Volvo B10M †
ADC 424	AEC Q	Bristol MW6G	MCW Metroliner
ADC 426		Leyland Royal Tiger *	

* Vehicles purchased primarily for Royal Blue relief work and painted accordingly but with Western National fleetnames.
† Vehicles owned by Trathens of Yelverton and used on National Express services operated jointly with Western National Ltd.

Below right: Requiem for a Bristol MW6G. For those who can bear to look, this 1960-vintage ECW 39-seater, No 2251 (618 DDV), new to Southern National, was withdrawn from its honourable Royal Blue service in 1973 and met its end at Rundle's scrapyard in Plymouth. All good things … Enough said! *C. L. Caddy*

Far right: Fortunately a happier fate awaited some Royal Blue coaches. One of the first batch of Bristol MW6Gs with ECW's re-styled coach body, Western National No 2270 (253 KTA) was the only coach allotted to the Royal Blue fleet proper in 1962, although others delivered to SNOC/WNOC would join it later. Withdrawn from service in 1977, it was purchased for preservation by Mr C. B. Wheble of Leatherhead, and, restored to its former glory, was photographed at the Bristol Rally in 1978. *M. S. Curtis*

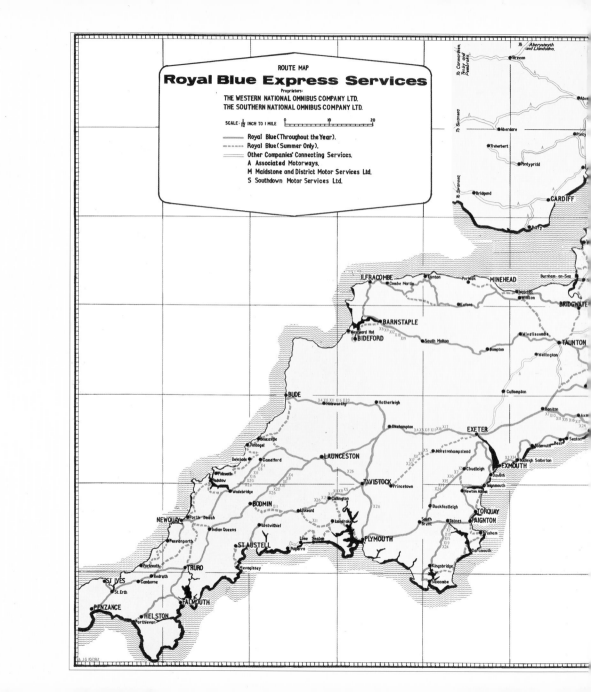

ROUTE MAP

Royal Blue Express Services

Proprietors:

THE WESTERN NATIONAL OMNIBUS COMPANY LTD.
THE SOUTHERN NATIONAL OMNIBUS COMPANY LTD.

SCALE: 1/12 INCH TO 1 MILE   0 — 10 — 20

— Royal Blue (Throughout the Year).
--- Royal Blue (Summer Only).
— Other Companies' Connecting Services.
A Associated Motorways.
M Maidstone and District Motor Services Ltd.
S Southdown Motor Services Ltd.